W9-COV-292

The
Pastor's Companion

The
Pastor's Companion

✠

AUTHORIZED BY THE SYNODS CONSTITUTING
THE EVANGELICAL LUTHERAN
SYNODICAL CONFERENCE OF NORTH AMERICA

✠

Oh, come, let us worship the Lord

CONCORDIA PUBLISHING HOUSE
Saint Louis, Missouri

ISBN 0-570-03650-**X**

TABLE OF CONTENTS

[V]

THE ORDER OF

HOLY BAPTISM

THE BAPTISM OF INFANTS
(WITH SPONSORS)

✠

PART ONE

(At the Lowest Chancel Step)

DEARLY BELOVED: (We learn from the Word of God that all men from the fall of Adam are conceived and born in sin and so are under the wrath of God and would be lost forever unless delivered by our Lord Jesus Christ.

This child, then, is also by nature sinful and under the wrath of God. But the Father of all mercy and grace hath promised and sent His Son Jesus Christ, who hath borne the sins of the whole world and redeemed and saved little children, no less than others, from sin, death, and everlasting condemnation. He also commanded that little children should be brought to Him and graciously received and blessed them.

Wherefore I beseech you out of Christian love to intercede for *this child,* to bring *him* to the Lord Jesus, and to ask for *him* the forgiveness of sin and the grace and salvation of Christ's kingdom, nowise doubting that our dear Lord favorably regardeth such work of love and certainly heareth our prayers. And)

Forasmuch as our Lord hath commanded Baptism, saying to His disciples in the last chapter of Matthew: Go ye, therefore, and teach all nations, baptizing them in the name of

the Father and of the Son and of the Holy Ghost; and also
hath given promise in the last chapter of Mark: He that
believeth and is baptized shall be saved; forasmuch, also, as
the holy Apostles of the Lord have written: The promise
is unto you and to your children, and again: Baptism doth
also now save us: it is meet and right that, in obedience to
His command and trusting in His promise, you should bring
this child to be baptized in His name.

❡ The Exhortation to the Sponsors (see page 4) may be read at this
place or, with slight changes in wording, at the close of the entire act,
after the concluding Prayer.

❡ Then the Minister may make the sign of the cross on the child's
forehead and breast, saying:

RECEIVE THE SIGN of the holy cross, both upon the forehead ✠ and upon the breast ✠, in token that thou hast been
redeemed by Christ the Crucified.

Let us pray.

❡ One or more of the following Prayers may be used.

1

ALMIGHTY AND ETERNAL GOD, Father of our Lord Jesus
Christ, we pray Thee, bestow upon *this N.,* here presented
for Holy Baptism, Thine everlasting grace through regeneration by the Holy Ghost. Receive *him,* O Lord, according
to Thy word and promise: Ask, and it shall be given you;
seek, and ye shall find; knock, and it shall be opened unto
you; and grant that *he* may obtain the everlasting blessing
of this heavenly washing and come to the Kingdom which
Thou hast promised; through Jesus Christ, our Lord. Amen.

2

LORD, holy Father, almighty, eternal God, from whom cometh down every good gift and every perfect gift with the light of Thy truth, we pray Thy merciful goodness that Thou wouldest bestow Thy blessing upon *this child,* here presented for Holy Baptism, that *he* may be enlightened with the light of Thy knowledge unto eternal salvation. Purify and sanctify *him,* give *him* the right understanding, that *he* may be made worthy of receiving the grace of Thy Baptism and that *he* may have the firm hope of final redemption through faith in Thy promises; through Jesus Christ, our Lord. Amen.

3

ALMIGHTY AND EVERLASTING GOD, who according to Thy righteous judgment didst destroy the unbelieving world by the Flood and according to Thy great mercy didst save faithful Noah and his family; who didst drown obdurate Pharaoh with all his host in the Red Sea and didst safely lead Thy people Israel through the midst thereof, prefiguring thereby this washing of Thy Holy Baptism; and who, by the Baptism of Thy beloved Son, our Lord Jesus Christ, didst sanctify and ordain Jordan and all waters for a saving flood and an abundant washing away of sin, we beseech Thee, of Thine infinite mercy, to look with favor upon *this child* and to bless *him* in the Spirit with true faith that, by this salutary flood, there may be drowned and destroyed in *him* all that *he* hath inherited from Adam and *himself* added thereto; and that, being separated from the number of the unbelieving, *he* may be securely kept in the holy ark of the Christian Church and ever serve Thy name with fervent spirit and joyful hope, to the end that, together with all believers, *he* may be accounted worthy to attain to everlasting life; through Jesus Christ, our Lord. Amen.

THE LESSON

HEAR THE HOLY GOSPEL of St. Mark which saith: And they brought young children to Jesus, that He should touch them; and His disciples rebuked those that brought them. But when Jesus saw it, He was much displeased and said unto them: Suffer the little children to come unto Me, and forbid them not, for of such is the Kingdom of God. Verily, I say unto you: Whosoever shall not receive the Kingdom of God as a little child, he shall not enter therein. And He took them up in His arms, put His hands upon them, and blessed them.

EXHORTATION TO THE SPONSORS

IT ALSO BEHOOVES you as sponsors, while confessing in this sacred act the faith of the Christian Church in the Triune God, in whose name *this child* is to be baptized, to bear witness publicly in the *child's* stead that by Holy Baptism as a means of grace *he* obtains and possesses the saving faith in the one true God and renounces the devil and his wicked works. Moreover, after *this child* has been baptized, you should at all times remember *him* in your prayers, put *him* in mind of *his* Baptism, and, as much as in you lies, lend your counsel and aid (especially if *he* should lose *his* parents), that *he* may be brought up in the true knowledge and fear of God,

℄ Either:

According to the teachings of the Lutheran Church and faithfully keep the baptismal covenant unto the end.

℄ Or:

And be taught the holy Ten Commandments, the Christian Creed, and the Lord's Prayer; and that, as *he* grows in years, you place in *his* hands the Holy Scriptures, bring *him* to the services of God's house, and provide for *his* further instruction in the Christian faith, that, abiding in the covenant of *his* Baptism and in communion with the Church, *he* may be brought up to lead a godly life until the day of Jesus Christ.

This, then, you intend gladly and willingly to do?
Yes.

MAY GOD ENABLE YOU both to will and to do this charitable work and with His grace fulfill what we are unable to do.

IN ORDER to implore the blessing of our Lord Jesus Christ upon *this child,* let us pray:

❦ Then the Minister, laying his right hand upon the head of the child, shall say, and the Sponsors and all present may say with him:

OUR FATHER who art in heaven. Hallowed be Thy name. Thy kingdom come. Thy will be done on earth as it is in heaven. Give us this day our daily bread. And forgive us our trespasses, as we forgive those who trespass against us. And lead us not into temptation. But deliver us from evil. For Thine is the kingdom and the power and the glory forever and ever. Amen.

❦ Then the Minister shall say:

THE LORD preserve thy coming in and thy going out from this time forth and even forevermore ✠ .

PART TWO
(At the Font)

❡ Then may the Minister say to the Sponsors:

DEAR CHRISTIAN FRIENDS AND SPONSORS: I now ask you to answer, in the name and in the stead of *this child*, the questions which I shall now address to *him*, to signify thereby what God in and through Baptism works in *him*.

❡ Then shall the Minister say:

N., DOST THOU RENOUNCE the devil and all his works and all his ways?

I do.

DOST THOU BELIEVE in God the Father Almighty, Maker of heaven and earth?

I do.

DOST THOU BELIEVE in Jesus Christ, His only Son, our Lord; Who was conceived by the Holy Ghost, Born of the Virgin Mary; Suffered under Pontius Pilate, Was crucified, dead, and buried; He descended into hell; The third day He rose again from the dead; He ascended into heaven And sitteth on the right hand of God the Father Almighty; From thence He shall come to judge the quick and the dead?

I do.

DOST THOU BELIEVE in the Holy Ghost; The holy Christian Church, the communion of saints; The forgiveness of sins; The resurrection of the body; And the life everlasting?

I do.

WILT THOU BE BAPTIZED into this Christian faith?
I will.

¶ Then shall the Minister apply water three times upon the head of the child as he names each Person of the Holy Trinity:

N., I baptize thee in the name of the Father and of the Son and of the Holy Ghost✠ . Amen.

¶ Then the Minister, laying his right hand upon the head of the child, shall say:

ALMIGHTY GOD, the Father of our Lord Jesus Christ, who hath begotten thee again of water and of the Spirit and hath forgiven thee all thy sins, strengthen thee with His grace unto life everlasting. Amen.

Peace be with thee✠ .

¶ The Minister, having proceeded to the altar, may add:

LET us pray:

Almighty and most merciful God and Father, we thank and praise Thee that Thou dost graciously preserve and extend Thy Church and hast granted *this child* the new birth in Holy Baptism and made *him a member* of Thy dear Son, our Lord Jesus Christ, and *an heir* of Thy heavenly kingdom. We humbly beseech Thee that, as *he* hath now become Thy *child,* Thou wouldst keep *him* in *his* baptismal grace, that, according to all Thy good pleasure, *he* may be faithfully brought up to lead a godly life to the praise and honor of Thy holy name and finally, with all Thy saints, obtain the promised inheritance in heaven, through Jesus Christ, our Lord. Amen.

THE ORDER OF

HOLY BAPTISM

THE BAPTISM OF INFANTS
(WITHOUT SPONSORS)

DEARLY BELOVED: In bringing *this child* to Baptism you are observing the will of the Lord, who commanded Baptism, saying in the last chapter of Matthew: Go ye, therefore, and teach all nations, baptizing them in the name of the Father and of the Son and of the Holy Ghost. We should, indeed, value this Sacrament highly, particularly since it is the only means of grace God has given us for little children. Little children, though seemingly innocent, are by birth and nature sinful, and without forgiveness would be lost forever. We know that God gave His Son into death to atone for the sins of all, that whosoever believeth in Him should not perish, but have everlasting life. But since little children are as yet unable to understand the Gospel, faith cannot be worked in them by telling them of Christ. We can never sufficiently thank God, therefore, that He has made Baptism a means whereby He works in little children with His divine grace, turning their hearts to faith, cleansing away their sins, and receiving them into His kingdom. The simple act of Baptism has such wonderful power because the almighty God Himself works in it through His word. Baptism is not simple water only, but it is the water comprehended in God's command and connected with God's word. The divine word makes Baptism what Paul calls it, Titus 3, the washing of regeneration and renewing of the Holy Ghost. For this reason Christ saith in the last chapter of Mark: He that believeth and is baptized shall be saved.

It is meet and right, therefore, that we should here, in the sight of God, administer and employ this blessed Sacrament in the fear of God, with due reverence, and with sincere devotion.

Receive the sign of the holy cross, both upon the forehead ✠ and upon the breast ✠ , in token that thou hast been redeemed by Christ the Crucified.

Hear the holy Gospel of St. Mark which saith: And they brought young children to Jesus, that He should touch them; and His disciples rebuked those that brought them. But when Jesus saw it, He was much displeased and said unto them: Suffer the little children to come unto Me, and forbid them not, for of such is the Kingdom of God. Verily, I say unto you: Whosoever shall not receive the Kingdom of God as a little child, he shall not enter therein. And He took them up in His arms, put His hands upon them, and blessed them.

In order to ask this blessing of our Lord Jesus Christ upon *this child*, let us pray:

Almighty and most merciful God, whose promises are unto us and unto our children, we heartily beseech Thee to look upon *this child* with Thy tender mercy and to renew *him* by Thy Holy Spirit in the Sacrament of Baptism, that *he* may be Thy *child* and *an heir* of everlasting life; through Jesus Christ, our Lord. Amen.

Our Father who art in heaven. Hallowed be Thy name. Thy kingdom come. Thy will be done on earth as it is in heaven. Give us this day our daily bread. And forgive us our trespasses, as we forgive those who trespass against us. And lead us not into temptation. But deliver us from evil. For Thine is the kingdom and the power and the glory forever and ever. Amen.

The Lord preserve thy coming in and thy going out from this time forth and even forevermore ✠.

Let us now confess our Christian faith, into which *this child* is to be baptized:

I believe in God the Father Almighty, Maker of heaven and earth.

And in Jesus Christ, His only Son, our Lord; Who was conceived by the Holy Ghost, Born of the Virgin Mary; Suffered under Pontius Pilate, Was crucified, dead, and buried; He descended into hell; The third day He rose again from the dead; He ascended into heaven And sitteth on the right hand of God the Father Almighty; From thence He shall come to judge the quick and the dead.

I believe in the Holy Ghost; The holy Christian Church, the communion of saints; The forgiveness of sins; The resurrection of the body; And the life everlasting. Amen.

N., I baptize thee in the name of the Father and of the Son and of the Holy Ghost ✠. Amen.

Almighty God, the Father of our Lord Jesus Christ, who hath begotten thee again of water and of the Spirit and hath forgiven thee all thy sins, strengthen thee with His grace unto life everlasting. Amen.

Peace be with thee ✠.

Let us pray:

We thank Thee, gracious Father, that Thou hast received *this child* through Holy Baptism into the covenant and kingdom of Thy grace, in which we have forgiveness of sin and everlasting life.   Grant, we beseech Thee, that, being buried with Christ in Baptism, *he* may be dead unto sin and made alive unto righteousness, that in the end, together with *his* parents and all saints, *he* may obtain the promised inheritance in heaven; through Jesus Christ, our Lord. Amen.

THE ORDER OF

HOLY BAPTISM

THE RATIFICATION OF LAY BAPTISM

✠

℞ If the Minister be uncertain whether the child has been baptized, he shall baptize it according to the Common Form.

℞ The following Order assumes the presence in the sanctuary of the child, the person who baptized the child, together with the witnesses of the lay Baptism.

℞ If Sponsors are desired, the proper questions to the Sponsors are asked after the fact of Baptism has been publicly established.

BELOVED IN THE LORD: *This child,* on account of extreme illness, hath received emergency Baptism. But God, the Lord, in His great mercy, hath preserved *his* life, and we have come here to be assured by public ratification, in due Christian order, that *this child* hath been baptized properly in accordance with the Word of God and that *his* Baptism was a valid Baptism. I, therefore, ask you, the baptizer, in the presence of God and this assembly:

HATH *this child* been baptized?

Yes.

BY WHOM was *he* baptized?

I, N., baptized the child.

WITH WHAT was *he* baptized?

With water.

WITH WHICH WORDS was *he* baptized?
With the words: "I baptize thee in the name of the Father and of the Son and of the Holy Ghost."

WHO was present at the time?
N. and N. were present.

❡ The Minister now addresses the witnesses:

DO YOU TESTIFY that all was done as is here said?
Yes.

WHAT NAME did the *child* receive in Baptism?
The name N.

❡ If the child has not been named, the Minister says:

HOW shall *this child* be named?
It is to be named N.

FORASMUCH, then, as you have done this in the name and upon the command of our Lord, you have done what was meet and right; for little children need the grace of our Lord Jesus Christ, who also graciously encouraged the bringing of them to Him, as we are comfortably assured in the tenth chapter of the Gospel according to St. Mark, where it saith: And they brought young children to Him, that He should touch them. And His disciples rebuked those that brought them. But when Jesus saw it, He was much displeased and said unto them: Suffer the little children to come unto Me, and forbid them not, for of such is the Kingdom of God. Verily, I say unto you: Whosoever shall not receive the Kingdom of God as a little child, he shall not enter therein. And He took them up in His arms, put His hands upon them, and blessed them.

From these words of the Lord Jesus we may be confident that *this child* also hath been received into the Kingdom of Grace.

❦ The Minister now addresses the Sponsors as follows:

IT ALSO BEHOOVES you as sponsors to bear witness publicly in the *child's* stead that by Holy Baptism as a means of grace *he* hath obtained and possesses the saving faith in the one true God and renounces the devil and his wicked works. Moreover, you should at all times remember *him* in your prayers, put *him* in mind of *his* Baptism, and, as much as in you lies, lend your counsel and aid (especially if *he* should lose *his* parents), that *he* may be brought up in the true knowledge and fear of God, according to the teachings of the Lutheran Church, and faithfully keep the baptismal covenant unto the end. This, then, you intend gladly and willingly to do?

Yes.

MAY GOD ENABLE you both to will and to do this charitable work and with His grace fulfill what we are unable to do. Amen.

❦ The Minister shall say:

LET US CONFESS the Christian faith in which *this child* has been baptized:

I believe in God the Father Almighty, Maker of heaven and earth.

And in Jesus Christ, His only Son, our Lord; Who was conceived by the Holy Ghost, Born of the Virgin Mary; Suffered under Pontius Pilate, Was crucified, dead, and buried; He descended into hell; The third day He rose again from the dead; He ascended into heaven And sitteth on the right hand of God the Father Almighty; From thence He shall come to judge the quick and the dead.

I believe in the Holy Ghost; The holy Christian Church, the communion of saints; The forgiveness of sins; The resurrection of the body; And the life everlasting. Amen.

¶ The Minister, laying his hand upon the head of the child, shall then say:

OUR FATHER who art in heaven. Hallowed be Thy name. Thy kingdom come. Thy will be done on earth as it is in heaven. Give us this day our daily bread. And forgive us our trespasses, as we forgive those who trespass against us. And lead us not into temptation. But deliver us from evil. For Thine is the kingdom and the power and the glory forever and ever. Amen.

Almighty God, the Father of our Lord Jesus Christ, who hath begotten thee again of water and of the Spirit and hath forgiven thee all thy sins, strengthen thee with His grace unto everlasting life. Amen.

Peace be with thee ✠ .

Let us pray:

Almighty and most merciful God and Father, we thank and praise Thee that Thou dost graciously preserve and extend Thy Church and hast granted to *this child* the new birth in Holy Baptism and made *him a member* of Thy dear Son, our Lord Jesus Christ, and *an heir* of Thy heavenly kingdom. We humbly beseech Thee that, as *he* hath become Thy *child*, Thou wouldst keep *him* in *his* baptismal grace, that, according to all Thy good pleasure, *he* may be faithfully brought up to lead a godly life to the praise and honor of Thy holy name and finally, with all Thy saints, obtain the promised inheritance in heaven, through Jesus Christ, our Lord. Amen.

(Or:

O ALMIGHTY GOD and Father of our Lord Jesus Christ, we thank Thee that Thou didst receive *this child* into Thy favor, and we beseech Thee to strengthen *him* by Thy Holy Spirit, that *he* may grow and increase in the new life to which Thou hast begotten *him* again. Grant that to this end *his* parents and all of us may faithfully serve Thee in *this child,* so that, as *a* living *member* of Thy Church, *he* may bring forth much fruit to the praise and honor of Thy holy name; through Jesus Christ, our Lord. Amen.

THE ORDER OF

HOLY BAPTISM

THE BAPTISM OF ADULTS

———————————— ✠ ————————————

❡ When an adult person is baptized, it is not necessary for him to receive Confirmation.

❡ When a person who has not been baptized in infancy desires to confess his faith in Christ and to receive Holy Baptism, he shall first be instructed in the Christian faith as it is set forth in the Small Catechism.

❡ The Baptism of adults shall be administered in the church, in the presence of the Congregation, except in cases of urgent necessity. When administered privately, public announcement of the Baptism shall be made at the next service of the Congregation.

❡ There may be held an Address and a brief Examination of the person to be baptized, and then the Minister may say:

D EARLY BELOVED: Our Lord and Savior Jesus Christ said to Nicodemus: Except a man be born of water and of the Spirit, he cannot enter into the Kingdom of God. That which is born of the flesh is flesh; and that which is born of the Spirit is spirit. All men, from the fall of Adam, being conceived and born in sin, are under the wrath of God and would be lost forever, had not the Father of all mercy and grace given His only-begotten Son Jesus Christ for the blotting out of our sins. In order that all men might come to the knowledge of the truth as it is in Christ Jesus, He has entrusted to His Church the means of grace for our salvation, saying, in the last chapter of Matthew: Go ye, therefore, and teach all nations, baptizing them in the name of the Father and of the

Son and of the Holy Ghost; teaching them to observe all things whatsoever I have commanded you: and again, in the last chapter of Mark: Go ye into all the world, and preach the Gospel to every creature. He that believeth and is baptized shall be saved; but he that believeth not shall be damned.

Whereas, then, in obedience to Christ's command and trusting in His promise, after due instruction in the principal doctrines of the Christian religion, *this person* desires to be baptized, let us call upon our heavenly Father to grant *him* all the promised blessings of the Sacrament, and pray:

O almighty and everlasting God, we bless Thee for Thy great mercy in calling *this* Thy *servant* unto faith in Thee, and we beseech Thee, remove from *him* all blindness of heart, and open unto *him* the gates of Thy mercy, that, by the washing of regeneration and renewing of the Holy Ghost, the life which has already been begun in *him* may be increased, strengthened, and confirmed, and *he* may be sealed unto eternal life, growing daily in grace, fighting the good fight of faith, and being steadfast and unmovable unto the end; through Jesus Christ, Thy dear Son, our Lord. Amen.

❡ The Catechumen shall then kneel, and the Minister shall place his hand on his head and pray:

OUR FATHER who art in heaven. Hallowed be Thy name. Thy kingdom come. Thy will be done on earth as it is in heaven. Give us this day our daily bread. And forgive us our trespasses, as we forgive those who trespass against us. And lead us not into temptation. But deliver us from evil. For Thine is the kingdom and the power and the glory forever and ever. Amen.

The Lord preserve thy coming in and thy going out from this time forth and even forevermore ✠.

❧ The Catechumen shall rise.

N., I now ask thee in the presence of God and these witnesses to answer the following questions:

DOST THOU RENOUNCE the devil and all his works and all his ways?

I do.

DOST THOU BELIEVE in God the Father Almighty?

I believe in God the Father Almighty, Maker of heaven and earth.

DOST THOU BELIEVE in Jesus Christ?

I believe in Jesus Christ, His only Son, our Lord; Who was conceived by the Holy Ghost, Born of the Virgin Mary; Suffered under Pontius Pilate, Was crucified, dead, and buried; He descended into hell; The third day He rose again from the dead; He ascended into heaven And sitteth on the right hand of God the Father Almighty; From thence He shall come to judge the quick and the dead.

DOST THOU BELIEVE in the Holy Ghost?

I believe in the Holy Ghost; The holy Christian Church, the communion of saints; The forgiveness of sins; The resurrection of the body; And the life everlasting.

DOST THOU DESIRE to be baptized into this Christian faith?

I do so desire.

WILT THOU, then, continue steadfast in the true Christian faith as it is confessed by our Evangelical Lutheran Church, be diligent in the use of the means of grace, and lead a godly life, even unto the end?

I will, with the help of God.

❡ Then shall the Minister and the person to be baptized proceed to
the font, and the Minister shall baptize him with water, saying:

N., I baptize thee in the name of the Father and of the Son
and of the Holy Ghost ✠. Amen.

❡ The baptized person may kneel, and the Minister, laying his right
hand on his head, shall say:

THE ALMIGHTY GOD, the Father of our Lord Jesus Christ,
who hath begotten thee again of water and of the Spirit and
hath forgiven thee all thy sins, strengthen thee with His grace
unto everlasting life. Amen.

❡ The baptized person shall stand.

IN THE NAME of the Church of Christ, I also invite thee, as
a baptized and instructed *member* of the Evangelical Lutheran
Church and of this congregation, to participate with us in
the reception of the Lord's Supper, for the strengthening of
thy faith, for thy furtherance in holiness of life, and in testi-
mony of the communion of faith.   In token thereof receive
the hand of Christian fellowship.

   Peace be with thee ✠

   Let us pray:

   Heavenly Father, we give Thee hearty thanks that Thou
hast vouchsafed to call us to the knowledge of Thy grace and
to faith in Thee; and we beseech Thee, increase this knowledge, and confirm this faith in us ever more.   Bestow Thy
Holy Spirit upon *this* our *brother* in Christ, that, being born
again and made *an heir* of everlasting salvation through our
Lord Jesus Christ, *he* may continue to be Thy *servant* and
attain Thy promises; through the same our Lord Jesus Christ,
Thy Son, who liveth and reigneth with Thee, in the unity of
the Holy Spirit, world without end. Amen.

THE RITE OF

CONFIRMATION

✠

℄ In the regular Morning Service the Examination may be placed after the singing of a Hymn following the Apostles' Creed; in the Vespers, after the singing of a Hymn following the Lection.

THE EXAMINATION

℄ The following introductory paragraph may be read.

WHEN CHILDREN have attained such knowledge of the truths of the Christian religion as are contained in the Catechism that, pursuant to the injunction of St. Paul, 1 Cor. 11:28, they are able to examine themselves, they should no longer be kept from the Holy Supper. Before they receive the Holy Sacrament, however, they should be examined and confirmed in the presence of the assembled congregation.

℄ The Minister may introduce the Examination by the following or another suitable Address:

DEARLY BELOVED: Holy Baptism is the washing of regeneration and renewing of the Holy Ghost, which God shed on us abundantly through Jesus Christ, our Savior, that, being justified by His grace, we should be made heirs according to the hope of eternal life. Through this Sacrament, God receives little children into His covenant and Kingdom of Grace, working faith in them and making them members of Christ's Church and temples of His Holy Spirit.

And as God will not suffer His faithfulness to fail, but keep His covenant and mercy; even so He says to each of His own:

Be thou faithful unto death, and I will give thee a crown of life. To the end, however, that this purpose of God may be accomplished and children may grow in grace and Christian knowledge as they advance in years, the Lord gave commandment, saying to parents through the Apostle Paul: Bring up your children in the nurture and admonition of the Lord, and to the Church, even as unto Simon Peter: Feed My lambs.

In accordance, then, with Christ's command, children are instructed in the Christian faith. When they reach an age of discretion and understand the covenant entered into by them by the grace of God in Holy Baptism, they should daily give their hearts to God and let their eyes observe His ways. In particular, being able to examine themselves and to discern the Lord's body, they should for their furtherance in grace receive the Sacrament of Holy Communion with the Church of God.

To encourage such growth in Christian knowledge and faith, the rite of Confirmation is maintained in the Lutheran Church. The catechumens publicly make profession of the true faith, confirming the covenant made between them and God. The Christian congregation, or church, the dispenser of God's mysteries, having assured itself that the catechumens possess such knowledge of Christian doctrine as may give warrant of their worthy eating of the body and drinking of the blood of Christ, invites them to receive the Holy Supper and, with the laying on of hands, prays over them for the Holy Spirit of God, that they may grow in grace, be steadfast and unmovable in their profession, become fruitful in every good work, and in the end receive the crown of life.

These catechumens have here presented themselves for Confirmation. We shall now examine them in the chief parts of Christian doctrine, for the purpose of setting forth that they understand the faith they are about to profess.

❡ Then shall the Catechumens be briefly examined.

❡ A Hymn may then be sung, followed by the Sermon.

❡ If the Confirmation be held in a later service, this service shall be concluded in the usual manner.

THE CONFIRMATION

❡ The Order of Confirmation shall follow the General Prayer in the Morning Service; in the Vespers, the Hymn after the Sermon.

❡ When adults not previously baptized are included in the group of Catechumens, they shall receive the Sacrament of Holy Baptism according to the Order for the Baptism of Adults. It is not necessary for them to receive Confirmation.

❡ Then may the Minister address the Catechumens thus:

DEARLY BELOVED: When you were little children, you were received into God's covenant of grace in Holy Baptism. And now, having learned the meaning of this covenant from your instruction in the Word of God, you are gathered here before God and this Christian congregation publicly to make profession of your faith in the Triune God and to confirm your covenant with Him, to dedicate yourselves body and soul for time and for eternity to your God and Lord. (Others of you are to make this public profession and promise and then, in obedience to Christ's command, to receive the Sacrament of Holy Baptism.) Lift up your hearts with me, therefore, to the God of all grace, and cheerfully give answer to what, in the name of the Lord, as a minister of His holy Church, I now shall ask you.

DO YOU THIS DAY, in the presence of God and of this Christian congregation, confirm the solemn covenant which at your Baptism you made with the Triune God?
I do.

Do You, then, renounce the devil and all his works and all his ways?
I do.

Do You Believe in God the Father?
Yes, I believe in God the Father . . .

Do You Believe in God the Son?
Yes, I believe in Jesus Christ . . .

Do You Believe in God the Holy Ghost?
Yes, I believe in the Holy Ghost . . .

Do You Desire to be a member of the Evangelical Lutheran Church and of this congregation?
I do.

Do You Hold all the canonical books of the Bible to be the inspired Word of God, and the doctrine of the Evangelical Lutheran Church, drawn from the Bible, as you have learned to know it from Luther's Small Catechism, to be the true and correct one?
I do.

Do You Also, as a member of the Evangelical Lutheran Church, intend to continue steadfast in the confession of this Church, and suffer all, even death, rather than fall away from it?
I do so intend, with the help of God.

Finally, do you intend faithfully to conform all your life to the rule of the divine Word, to be diligent in the use of the means of grace, to walk as it becometh the Gospel of Christ, and in faith, word, and deed to remain true to the Triune God, even unto death?
I do so intend, by the grace of God.

¶ Then shall the Minister say:

G<small>IVE</small> now your hand at the Lord's altar, as a pledge of your promise, and, kneeling, receive His blessing.

¶ Then shall the Catechumens come forward — one by one, or in groups, as the Minister may have appointed — and, giving the Minister their right hand, kneel before the altar.

¶ Then shall the Minister, laying his hands upon each one separately, pronounce the name of the Catechumen and the Benediction, adding a Scripture passage as a memorial of Confirmation, saying:

N., God, the Father of our Lord Jesus Christ, give thee His Holy Spirit, the Spirit of wisdom and knowledge, of grace and prayer, of power and strength, of sanctification and the fear of God.

¶ Or:

N., The Father in heaven, for Jesus' sake, renew and increase in thee the gift of the Holy Ghost, to thy strengthening in faith, to thy growth in grace, to thy patience in suffering, and to the blessed hope of everlasting life.

¶ Or:

N., The God of all grace, who hath called us unto His eternal glory by Christ Jesus, make thee perfect, stablish, strengthen, settle thee, and keep thee through faith unto eternal life.

¶ Or:

N., The God of peace sanctify thee wholly; and may thy whole spirit and soul and body be preserved blameless unto the coming of our Lord Jesus Christ.

¶ Or:

N., May God, who hath begun the good work in thee, perform it until the day of our Lord Jesus Christ.

❡ Then shall the Minister say:

UPON this (these) your voluntary profession(s) and prom-
ise(s), I, in the name of the Church of Christ, invite and
welcome you, as a member (as members) of the Evangelical
Lutheran Church and of this congregation, to participate with
us in all the rights and privileges of the Evangelical Lutheran
Church, in the name of the Father and of the Son and of the
Holy Ghost.

❡ Then shall the Minister pronounce the Benediction:

THE LORD bless thee and keep thee.

The Lord make His face shine upon thee and be gracious
unto thee.

The Lord lift up His countenance upon thee and give thee
peace ✠.

❡ The group shall say:
Amen.

❡ Then shall the Minister invite the Congregation to make Intercession.
as follows:

SINCE it is God alone who worketh both to will and to do
of His good pleasure, it behooveth us, dear friends in Christ,
to call upon Him for these young members of this Christian
congregation, that He would graciously perform the good work
which He hath begun in them. Let us, therefore, (kneel
and) pray.

ALMIGHTY AND EVERLASTING GOD, who makest us both to
will and to do those things which are good and acceptable
unto Thy divine majesty, we make our humble supplications
unto Thee for these Thy servants. Let Thy fatherly hand,

we beseech Thee, ever be over them; let Thy Holy Spirit ever be with them; and so lead them in the knowledge and obedience of Thy Word that in the end they may obtain everlasting life, through our Lord Jesus Christ, who, with Thee and the Holy Ghost, liveth and reigneth, ever one God, world without end.

❦ The Congregation shall say:
  Amen.

❦ Or:

LORD GOD, heavenly Father, we thank and praise Thee for Thy great goodness in bringing these Thy servants to the knowledge of Thy Son Jesus Christ and the truth of the Gospel revealed through Him, and in enabling them both with the heart to believe and with the mouth to confess His name. We also entreat Thee to enlighten and strengthen them by Thy Holy Spirit, that they may daily increase in living faith, in godly fear, in patience under trials, in true knowledge of Thee, and in all other things profitable to their eternal salvation. Grant that, bringing forth the fruits of faith and love, they may continue steadfast and victorious unto the day when all who have fought the good fight of faith shall receive the crown of righteousness, through Jesus Christ, Thy Son, our Lord, who liveth and reigneth with Thee and the Holy Ghost, ever one God, world without end.

❦ Or:

ALMIGHTY AND EVERLIVING GOD, we thank Thee that Thou hast brought these Thy servants to Thy Son Jesus Christ in Holy Baptism, cleansed them by His blood, and buried them with Him by Baptism into His death. And we beseech Thee, of Thy great goodness, to renew in them the gift of the Holy

Ghost, that their hearts may be filled with the light of Thy Gospel. Increase in them pure knowledge and true faith, that they may firmly believe in Thee, the only true God, and in Jesus Christ, whom Thou hast sent, and ever cleave to Thee with steadfast confidence. Defend them from the power of darkness, and establish them in the Kingdom of Thy Son, wherein we have redemption and forgiveness of sins. Fill their hearts and minds with the peace of Christ, the joy of the Holy Spirit, and love to Thee and all mankind. Endow them plenteously with the gifts of Thy heavenly grace, that they may be led into all truth, mortify the deeds of the flesh, overcome the assaults and temptations of the Wicked One, and serve Thee in Thy Church in holiness and righteousness all their days; and that, together with all true believers, they may, with joyful hearts and watchful prayer and in soberness and godly living, hope and wait for the coming of the Savior, to the honor of Thy holy name, who livest and reignest with the Son and the Holy Ghost, ever one God, world without end.

℄ Or:

ALMIGHTY AND EVERLASTING GOD, the Author and Finisher of our faith, who, of Thine infinite mercy, hast added to Thy Church these Thy servants by causing them to be born again of water and the Holy Ghost and hast given them knowledge of their redemption in Christ and power to own and confess Thee in the presence of Thy people, we thank Thee for the great mercy Thou hast been pleased to show them, and beseech Thee, strengthen them by Thy Holy Spirit, and daily increase in them the manifold gifts of Thy grace, the spirit of wisdom and understanding, the spirit of counsel and might, the spirit of knowledge and of the fear of the Lord, that they may be kept in the Kingdom and covenant of Christ through faith unto everlasting life. Fortify them against the assaults of sin.

Let not Satan prevail against them. Keep them from the evil that is in the world. Help them to walk in the Spirit that they may not fulfill the lusts of the flesh, but serve Thee in holiness and righteousness all their days. Defend them from all heresy and schism, from all apostasy and unbelief. Make them faithful unto death that no man may take from them their crown. And grant that, continuing steadfast in faith and hope, they may at the end be found meet to be partakers of the inheritance of the saints in light; through Jesus Christ, Thy Son, our Lord, who liveth and reigneth with Thee and the Holy Ghost, ever one God, world without end.

❡ Then shall the Minister and the Congregation say:

Our Father who art in heaven. Hallowed be Thy name. Thy kingdom come. Thy will be done on earth as it is in heaven. Give us this day our daily bread. And forgive us our trespasses, as we forgive those who trespass against us. And lead us not into temptation. But deliver us from evil. For Thine is the kingdom and the power and the glory forever and ever. Amen.

❡ Then may be sung a Hymn.

❡ Then shall the Minister pronounce the Benediction upon the Congregation:

THE LORD bless thee and keep thee.

The Lord make His face shine upon thee and be gracious unto thee.

The Lord lift up His countenance upon thee and give thee peace ✠.

❡ The Congregation shall say or chant:

Amen.

SILENT PRAYER

THE RECEPTION OF

CONVERTS

✠

❡ In the regular Morning Service this Act may be placed immediately before the General Prayer; in the Matins or Vespers, after the Canticle; the Service being concluded in the usual way.

❡ The Minister, addressing the Congregation, shall say:

DEAR FRIENDS IN CHRIST: *N.*, here present, *desires* to become *a member* of the Evangelical Lutheran Church, being fully convinced that in this Church the Word of God is taught in its truth and purity and the Sacraments are administered according to their institution by Christ.

I, therefore, ask *thee, N.,* in the presence of God and of this congregation:

DOST *Thou* ACKNOWLEDGE and confess the teachings of the Evangelical Lutheran Church to be the true and unaltered teachings of the Word of God?

I do.

DOST *Thou*, THEREFORE, DESIRE, in sincere obedience to God, to be received by us into the communion of the Evangelical Lutheran Church and of this congregation?

I do.

DOST *Thou* INTEND to continue in the confession of this Church, to make diligent use of the means of grace, and to lead a sober, righteous, and godly life, even unto the end?

I do so intend, with the help of God.

Upon This *Thy* Promise, I, in the name of this congregation, give to *thee* the right hand of fellowship and love, acknowledging *thee* as *a member* of the Evangelical Lutheran Church, and inviting *thee* to join us in the reception of the Lord's Supper and to participate in all the other blessings of salvation which God has given to His Church, in the name of the Father and of the Son and of the Holy Ghost.

The grace of our Lord Jesus Christ be with *thee*, enabling *thee* to receive the truth in the love of it and to do the will of God from the heart, and keeping *thee* unto His kingdom and glory. Amen.

Peace be with *thee* ✠. Amen.

❧ The Minister, addressing the Congregation, shall say:

Dearly Beloved: *N.*, having become convinced that the doctrines of the Evangelical Lutheran Church are the very truth of God's holy Word, has declared *his* conviction before the pastor and church council of this congregation and *has* been received as *a member* of this congregation.   May the God of all grace, who has led *him* to see and confess the pure truth of the Gospel, preserve and strengthen *him* in true faith that *he* may continue steadfast unto the end and receive the crown of everlasting life! Amen.

❧ Then may follow a suitable Prayer or the General Prayer, and the Service shall be closed in the usual way.

THE RECEPTION OF

MEMBERS

BY TRANSFER

✠

¶ In the regular Morning Service this Act may be placed immediately before the General Prayer; in the Matins or Vespers, after the Canticle; the Service being concluded in the usual way.

¶ The Minister shall address the *person(s)* to be received as follows:

DEARLY BELOVED: *You are* here, as *members* of the Evangelical Lutheran Church, to become *members* of this congregation (or, to transfer *your* membership to this congregation). And whereas nothing has been shown to hinder *your* reception into communion with us, I ask *you,* in the presence of God and of this assembly:

Do you intend to submit to the government and discipline of this congregation, administered according to its established forms and order?

I do so intend.

¶ The Minister then gives his right hand, saying:

UPON THIS YOUR PROMISE, I, in the name of this congregation, give to *you* the right hand of fellowship and love and invite *you* to join us in the celebration of the Lord's Supper and to participate in all the rights and privileges of this congregation. The blessing of God Almighty, the Father, the Son, and the Holy Ghost, be upon *you* and remain with *you* forever. Amen.

Depart in peace.

THE ANNOUNCEMENT OF
EXCOMMUNICATION,
OF SELF-EXCLUSION,
AND OF REINSTATEMENT

✠

℩ In the case of Excommunication, Self-Exclusion, or Reinstatement, local custom will determine the time and the place for the Announcement, which may be made as follows.

EXCOMMUNICATION BY THE CONGREGATION

Beloved in Christ: It is my painful duty to make known to you that our fellow member, *N.*, was under discipline and, although repeatedly admonished from the Word of God, has manifested no evidence of true repentance. The assembled congregation has, therefore, excommunicated *him* until *he* give evidence of repentance. May the almighty and merciful God grant *him* grace to know *his* sin, work in *him* true repentance, and awaken *him* to reformation of life. Amen.

SELF-EXCLUSION

It Is My Painful Duty to make known to you that *N.*, being under discipline, has declared *his* withdrawal from this congregation. *He* has thereby deprived us of the opportunity to admonish *him* henceforth as a *brother;* and we are constrained to commit *his* cause to Him that judgeth righteously. May the Lord, of His great mercy, grant *him* knowledge of *his* sinful conduct that *he* may repent and return. Amen.

REINSTATEMENT

BELOVED IN CHRIST: Whereas *N.*, after being under excommunication for a time, has now, by the grace of God, given evidence of repentance, the congregation, in meeting assembled, has removed the excommunication from the said *N.* and has restored *him* to Christian fellowship in this congregation. May God, by His Holy Spirit, graciously enable *him* to continue steadfast in faith and godliness unto the end, through Jesus Christ, our Lord. Amen.

THE ORDER OF

A MARRIAGE

THE CONGREGATION PARTICIPATING

❧ The persons to be married having presented themselves at the entrance to the chancel, the man to the right of the woman, a suitable Hymn may be sung.

❧ The Minister shall say or chant:

IN THE NAME of the Father and of the Son and of the Holy Ghost.

❧ The Congregation shall say or chant:

Amen.

❧ The Minister shall read a suitable Scripture Lesson, such as John 2: 1-11 or Psalm 67 or Psalm 23. If the Minister reads a Psalm, the Congregation shall respond by singing the Gloria Patri.

❧ The Minister, standing before the bridal pair, at the entrance to the chancel, may give the Address. Then the Minister shall say:

DEARLY BELOVED: Whereas you desire to enter upon the holy estate of matrimony, ordained of God, and to be held in honor by all, it becometh you, with reverent minds, to hear what the Word of God teacheth concerning this estate:

The Lord God saith, It is not good that the man should be alone; I will make him an help meet for him.

Our Lord Jesus Christ saith: Have ye not read that He which made them at the beginning, made them male and female, and said, For this cause shall a man leave father and mother and shall cleave to his wife; and they twain shall be one flesh? Wherefore they are no more twain, but one flesh. What therefore God hath joined together, let not man put asunder.

The Apostle Paul, speaking by the Holy Ghost, saith: Husbands, love your wives, even as Christ also loved the Church, and gave Himself for it. So ought men to love their wives as their own bodies. He that loveth his wife loveth himself. For no man ever yet hated his own flesh, but nourisheth and cherisheth it, even as the Lord the Church. Wives, submit yourselves unto your own husbands as unto the Lord. For the husband is the head of the wife, even as Christ is the Head of the Church; and He is the Savior of the body. Therefore as the Church is subject unto Christ, so let the wives be to their own husbands in everything.

And although, by reason of sin, many a cross hath been laid upon this estate, nevertheless our gracious Father in heaven doth not forsake His children in an estate so holy and acceptable to Him, but is ever present with His bountiful blessings.

For thus saith the Lord in the Psalm: Blessed is everyone that feareth the Lord, that walketh in His ways. For thou shalt eat the labor of thine hands. Happy shalt thou be, and it shall be well with thee. Thy wife shall be as a fruitful vine by the sides of thine house; thy children like olive plants round about thy table. Behold, that thus shall the man be blessed that feareth the Lord. The Lord shall bless thee out of Zion; and thou shalt see the good of Jerusalem all the days of thy life. Yea, thou shalt see thy children's children and peace upon Israel.

Thus hath our heavenly Father sanctified the estate of

matrimony. He will ever bless therein all who love Him, trust in Him, and live in His fear, for Jesus' sake.

Dearly beloved, you have come here to be united into this holy estate, which consisteth in your mutual consent, sincerely and freely given; it behooveth you, then, to declare, in the presence of God and these witnesses, the sincere intent you both have.

❧ Then the Minister may say:

WHO GIVETH this woman to be married to this man?

❧ The father or another relative shall say:
   I do.

❧ Then shall the Minister say to the man:

N., wilt thou have this woman to be thy wedded wife, to live with her after God's ordinance in the holy estate of matrimony? Wilt thou love her, comfort her, honor her, and keep her in sickness and in health, and, forsaking all others, keep thee only unto her, so long as ye both shall live?

❧ The man shall say:
   I will.

❧ Then shall the Minister say to the woman:

N., wilt thou have this man to be thy wedded husband, to live with him after God's ordinance in the holy estate of matrimony? Wilt thou love him, comfort him, honor him, obey him, and keep him in sickness and in health, and, forsaking all others, keep thee only unto him, so long as ye both shall live?

℃ The woman shall say:

I will.

℃ Then may the Minister place the right hand of the woman in the right hand of the man. Then shall they loose their hands.

℃ Then shall the Minister precede the man and the woman to the altar. The veil of the woman shall be lifted. The man, facing the woman, shall take the right hand of the woman, facing him, and say after the Minister:

I, *N.,* in the presence of God and these witnesses, / take thee, *N.,* to be my wedded wife / and plight thee my troth / till death us do part.

℃ Then shall the woman, in like manner, say after the Minister:

I, *N.,* in the presence of God and these witnesses, / take thee, *N.,* to be my wedded husband / and plight thee my troth / till death us do part.

℃ If the wedding ring be used, the Minister shall now receive it and deliver it to the man to be put on the fourth finger of the woman's left hand.

℃ Then shall the man say, or if two rings be used, the man and the woman, in turn, shall say, after the Minister:

RECEIVE THIS RING / as a pledge and token / of wedded love and faithfulness.

℃ Then shall the Minister say:

MAY THE GIVING and receiving of this ring (these rings) ever be a symbol of the faithful and unselfish community of goods that you as husband and wife, in weal and woe, will cultivate without ceasing, and be a reminder of the excellent Christian virtues with which you will adorn your marriage. To this end may God bless you through the heavenly Bridegroom, Jesus Christ, our Lord.

❡ Then shall the Minister say:

JOIN your right hands.

❡ Then shall the Minister lay his right hand upon their hands and say:

FORASMUCH as *N.* and *N.* have consented together in holy wedlock and have declared the same before God and these witnesses, I pronounce them husband and wife in the name of the Father and of the Son and of the Holy Ghost ✠. Amen.

What therefore God hath joined together, let not man put asunder.

❡ Then shall they turn to face the altar and kneel, and the Minister shall bless them, saying:

MAY THE ALMIGHTY AND ETERNAL GOD look down from His exalted throne in heaven upon you with His favor and sanctify and bless you with the benediction first spoken to Adam and Eve in Paradise, that you may please Him both in body and soul, and live together in holy love until life's end.

The eternal God, the Father of our Lord Jesus Christ, bestow upon you His Holy Spirit and be with you and richly bless you forevermore. Amen.

❡ Or:

The God of Abraham, the God of Isaac, the God of Jacob, be with you and richly bless you forevermore. Amen.

❛ Then shall the man and the woman rise and stand facing the altar.
If no hymn is sung, they remain kneeling.

❛ Then may a suitable Hymn be sung.

❛ Then shall the man and the woman kneel.

❛ Then shall the Minister say or chant:

LET us pray:

Almighty, eternal God, our heavenly Father, who hast united
this man and this woman in the holy estate of matrimony,
grant them the grace to live therein according to Thy Word;
strengthen them in constant faithfulness and true love toward
each other; sustain and defend them amidst all trials and
temptations; and help them so to pass through this world
in faith towards Thee, in communion with Thy holy Church,
and in loving service one of the other, that they may ever
enjoy Thy heavenly benediction; through Jesus Christ, Thy
Son, our Lord, who liveth and reigneth with Thee and the
Holy Ghost, ever one God, world without end.

❛ The Congregation shall say or chant:

Amen.

❛ Then shall all say:

*Our Father who art in heaven.   Hallowed be Thy name.   Thy kingdom
come.   Thy will be done on earth as it is in heaven.   Give us this day
our daily bread.   And forgive us our trespasses, as we forgive those who
trespass against us.   And lead us not into temptation.   But deliver us
from evil.   For Thine is the kingdom and the power and the glory forever
and ever.   Amen.*

❡ Then shall the Minister say or chant the Benediction:

THE LORD bless thee and keep thee.

The Lord make His face shine upon thee and be gracious unto thee.

The Lord lift up His countenance upon thee and give thee peace ✠.

❡ Then shall the Congregation say or chant:
Amen.

SILENT PRAYER

THE ORDER OF

A MARRIAGE

THE CONGREGATION NOT PARTICIPATING

✠

℃ The persons to be married having presented themselves at the entrance of the chancel, the man on the right hand and the woman on his left, the Minister shall say:

DEARLY BELOVED: Forasmuch as you purpose to enter upon the holy estate of matrimony, which is to be held in honor by all, it becometh you to hear what the Word of God teacheth concerning this estate.

Know ye, therefore, that God Himself ordained marriage when He said:

It is not good that the man should be alone; I will make him an help meet for him. And the Lord God caused a deep sleep to fall upon Adam, and he slept; and He took one of his ribs and closed up the flesh instead thereof; and the rib which the Lord God had taken from man made He a woman and brought her unto the man. And Adam said: This is now bone of my bones and flesh of my flesh; she shall be called Woman, because she was taken out of Man. Therefore shall a man leave his father and his mother and shall cleave unto his wife, and they shall be one flesh.

Hear also what God hath commanded as touching the conduct of spouses toward each other:

Husbands, love your wives, even as Christ also loved the Church and gave Himself for it, that He might sanctify and cleanse it with the washing of water by the Word, that He might present it to Himself a glorious Church, not having spot or wrinkle or any such thing, but that it should be holy and without blemish.

So ought men to love their wives as their own bodies. He that loveth his wife loveth himself. For no man ever yet hated his own flesh, but nourisheth and cherisheth it, even as the Lord the Church.

Wives, submit yourselves unto your own husbands as unto the Lord. For the husband is the head of the wife, even as Christ is the Head of the Church; and He is the Savior of the body. Therefore as the Church is subject unto Christ, so let the wives be to their own husbands in everything.

Hear also the cross which by reason of sin God hath laid upon this estate:

Unto the woman He said: I will greatly multiply thy sorrow and thy conception; in sorrow thou shalt bring forth children; and thy desire shall be to thy husband, and he shall rule over thee. And unto Adam He said: Because thou hast hearkened unto the voice of thy wife and hast eaten of the tree of which I commanded thee, saying, Thou shalt not eat of it: cursed is the ground for thy sake; in sorrow shalt thou eat of it all the days of thy life; thorns also and thistles shall it bring forth to thee; and thou shalt eat the herb of the field; in the sweat of thy face shalt thou eat bread till thou return unto the ground; for out of it wast thou taken; for dust thou art, and unto dust shalt thou return.

Nevertheless, marriage is well pleasing to God and hath His blessings; for it is written:

God created man in His own image, in the image of God created He him; male and female created He them. And God blessed them, and God said unto them: Be fruitful, and multiply, and replenish the earth, and subdue it; and have dominion over the fish of the sea, and over the fowl of the air, and over every living thing that moveth upon the earth. And God saw everything that He had made, and, behold, it was very good. Therefore Solomon also saith: Whoso findeth a wife findeth a good thing and obtaineth favor of the Lord.

The Psalm, also, saith of the man:

Blessed is everyone that feareth the Lord, that walketh in His ways. For thou shalt eat the labor of thine hands. Happy shalt thou be, and it shall be well with thee. Thy wife shall be as a fruitful vine by the sides of thine house, thy children like olive plants round about thy table. Behold, that thus shall the man be blessed that feareth the Lord. The Lord shall bless thee out of Zion; and thou shalt see the good of Jerusalem all the days of thy life. Yea, thou shalt see thy children's children and peace upon Israel.

Thus God hath sanctified marriage and will continue to bless therein all who trust in Him and live in His fear; for Christ, having atoned for our sin, hath hallowed even the crosses of those who believe in Him.

Into this holy estate you now come to be united, and that all men may know your mutual consent in holy wedlock to have been sincerely and freely given, it behooveth you to declare, in the presence of God and these witnesses, the sincere intent you both have.

These two persons have come hither to be made one in this holy estate. If there be any here present who can show just cause why they may not lawfully be joined in marriage, let him now speak, or ever after hold his peace.

Forasmuch, then, as nothing has been shown to hinder this marriage, I ask you:

N., wilt thou have N., here present, to be thy wedded wife? Wilt thou love, honor, and cherish her, and keep with her this bond of wedlock holy and unbroken till death you do part? If so, declare it before God and these witnesses by saying, I will.

I will.

N., wilt thou have N., here present, to be thy wedded husband? Wilt thou love, honor, cherish, and obey him, and keep with him this bond of wedlock holy and unbroken till death you do part? If so, declare it before God and these witnesses by saying, I will.

I will.

❡ If the wedding ring be used, the Minister shall now receive it and deliver it to the man to be put on the fourth finger of the woman's left hand. The bride and the groom shall face each other.

❡ Then shall the man say, or if two rings be used, the man and the woman, in turn, shall say, after the Minister:

RECEIVE THIS RING / as a pledge and token / of wedded love and faithfulness.

❡ Or the Minister may say:

EXCHANGE RINGS as a pledge and token of wedded love and faithfulness.

❡ Then shall the Minister say:

JOIN your right hands.

❡ Here the Minister may direct the man to say after him:

I, N., in the presence of God and this assembly, / take thee, N., to be my wedded wife, / and plight thee my troth in every duty, / not to part from thee / till death us do part.

❡ In like manner may the woman also say after the Minister:

I, *N.*, in the presence of God and this assembly, / take thee,
N., to be my wedded husband, / and plight thee my troth in
every duty, / not to part from thee / till death us do part.

❡ Then shall the Minister say:

WHAT GOD HATH JOINED TOGETHER, let not man put
asunder. And forasmuch as *N.* and *N.* have consented together in holy wedlock and have witnessed the same before
God and this assembly (these witnesses), I pronounce them
husband and wife, in the name of the Father and of the Son
and of the Holy Ghost ✠. Amen.

❡ Then shall the persons married kneel for prayer, and the Minister
shall say:

ALMIGHTY GOD, who didst create man and woman, and didst
join them together in marriage, thereby signifying the mystery of the union betwixt Thy Son Jesus Christ and His Bride,
the Church: we beseech Thine infinite goodness, let not this
Thy blessed work and ordinance be set aside or brought to
naught, but graciously protect and preserve it. Especially let
Thy blessing rest upon these Thy servants; so rule them by
Thy Holy Spirit that they may live together to Thy glory
and to their own welfare in this life and in that which is to
come. Keep them in Thy favor, and bring them unto everlasting life; through Jesus Christ, our Lord. Amen.

❡ Or:

LORD, our God, our Helper and our Comforter in time and
in eternity, graciously look upon these Thy servants, who
according to Thy holy ordinance have entered the covenant
of wedded love and troth. Do Thou bless them, and so guide

them by Thy Holy Spirit that in all things Thy good and gracious will may be done in them. May they let the Word of Christ dwell in them richly, and do Thou make their home and their hearts Thy dwelling place. Grant that their souls be united in Christ Jesus unto one mind by love, and may their mutual true affection never know doubt or change. Do Thou bless them in each other, and enable them in wisdom and meekness to bear with patience each other's infirmities. Prosper the work of their hands, and crown their lives with Thy loving-kindness and tender mercies. Let even their crosses and afflictions yield them the peaceable fruit of righteousness as an abiding blessing, and teach them, in everything by prayer and supplication with thanksgiving, to make their requests known unto Thee. And when in steadfast faith they have finished their pilgrimage on earth, give them a dwelling place with Thee in heavenly joy; for the sake of Jesus Christ, Thy Son, our Lord.

OUR FATHER who art in heaven. Hallowed be Thy name. Thy kingdom come. Thy will be done on earth as it is in heaven. Give us this day our daily bread. And forgive us our trespasses, as we forgive those who trespass against us. And lead us not into temptation. But deliver us from evil. For Thine is the kingdom and the power and the glory forever and ever. Amen.

❡ Then shall the Minister pronounce the Benediction:

THE LORD bless thee and keep thee.

The Lord make His face shine upon thee and be gracious unto thee.

The Lord lift up His countenance upon thee and give thee peace ✠. Amen.

THE ORDER OF

A MARRIAGE

A SHORT FORM

---✠---

❡ The persons to be married having presented themselves at the entrance of the chancel, the man on the right hand and the woman on his left, the Minister shall say:

DEARLY BELOVED: We are assembled here in the presence of God and these witnesses to join together this man and this woman in holy matrimony, which was instituted by God for the welfare and happiness of mankind, blessed by our Lord Jesus Christ, and likened by St. Paul to the mystical union subsisting between Christ and His Church, and which is to be held in honor among all men. Wherefore those who purpose to enter this holy estate should do so with a profound sense of the seriousness of the obligations they are about to assume, duly and devoutly weighing what Holy Scripture teaches concerning husbands and wives, and bearing in mind that the vow and covenant once made may not be broken. Our Savior has declared that a man shall forsake his father and mother and cleave unto his wife, for they twain shall be one flesh. By His Apostles He has instructed those who enter into wedlock to cherish mutual esteem and love; to bear with each other's infirmities and weaknesses; to comfort each other in sickness, trouble, and sorrow; in honesty and industry to provide for each other and for their household in temporal things; to pray for and encourage each other in the things which pertain to God; and to live together as the heirs of the grace of life.

❡ Or:

[48]

DEARLY BELOVED: We are gathered together here in the sight of God to join together this man and this woman in holy matrimony, which is commended of St. Paul to be honorable among all men and therefore is not by any to be entered into unadvisedly or lightly, but reverently, discreetly, advisedly, soberly, and in the fear of God.

THESE TWO PERSONS have come hither to be made one in this holy estate. If there be any here present who can show just cause why they may not lawfully be joined in marriage, let him now speak or ever after hold his peace.

Forasmuch, then, as nothing has been shown to hinder this marriage, I ask you:

N., wilt thou have N., here present, to be thy wedded wife, to live together after God's ordinance in the holy estate of matrimony? Wilt thou love her, comfort her, honor her, and keep her in sickness and in health, and, forsaking all others, keep thee only unto her so long as ye both shall live?
I will.

N., wilt thou have N., here present, to be thy wedded husband, to live together after God's ordinance in the holy estate of matrimony? Wilt thou love him, comfort him, honor and obey him, and keep him in sickness and in health, and, forsaking all others, keep thee only unto him so long as ye both shall live?
I will.

❡ Then the Minister may say:

WHO GIVETH this woman to be married to this man?

4

❡ Then the father or another relative shall say:

    I do.

❡ The father or another relative of the woman shall with his right hand put her right hand into the right hand of the Minister, who shall cause the man with his right hand to take the woman by her right hand and to say after him, as they face each other:

I, *N.,* in the presence of God and this assembly, / take thee, *N.,* to be my wedded wife, / and plight thee my troth in every duty, / not to part from thee / till death us do part.

❡ Then shall they loose their right hands. Then shall the Minister with his right hand cause the woman with her right hand to take the man by his right hand and shall likewise say after the Minister:

I, *N.,* in the presence of God and this assembly, / take thee, *N.,* to be my wedded husband, / and plight thee my troth in every duty, / not to part from thee / till death us do part.

❡ Then shall they again loose their right hands, and if the wedding ring be used, the Minister shall now ask for it and say:

IN TOKEN of your vows thus mutually plighted, you, *N.,* give, and you, *N.,* receive the wedding ring.

❡ Then the Minister, taking the ring with his right hand, shall deliver it to the man, who shall then put it on the fourth finger of the woman's left hand, and the Minister shall say, and the man shall say after him:

RECEIVE THIS RING / as a pledge and token / of wedded love and faithfulness.

❡ Or:

WITH THIS RING I thee wed, *N.,* / in the name of the Father and of the Son and of the Holy Ghost. Amen.

❡ Or the Minister may say (if two rings be used, each one may say after him):

WITH THIS RING I thee wed, *N.*, / in the name of the Father and of the Son and of the Holy Ghost. Amen.

❡ Or:

EXCHANGE RINGS as a pledge and token of wedded love and faithfulness.

❡ Then shall the Minister say:

JOIN your right hands.

❡ Then shall the Minister lay his right hand upon their hands and say:

FORASMUCH as *N.* and *N.* have consented together in holy wedlock and have witnessed the same before God and this assembly (these witnesses) (and thereto have given and pledged their troth, each to the other), and have declared the same (by giving and receiving a ring, and) by joining hands: I pronounce them husband and wife in the name of the Father and of the Son and of the Holy Ghost ✠. Amen.

What, therefore, God hath joined together let not man put asunder.

❡ Then shall the persons married kneel for prayer, and the Minister shall say:

O ETERNAL GOD, Creator and Preserver of all mankind, Giver of all spiritual grace, the Author of everlasting life: send Thy blessing upon these Thy servants, this man and this woman, whom we bless in Thy name, that, living faithfully together, they may surely perform and keep the vow and covenant betwixt them made and may ever remain in perfect love and peace together, and so live in this life according to Thy laws that in the world to come they may have life everlasting; through Jesus Christ, our Lord.

Our Father who art in heaven. Hallowed be Thy name. Thy kingdom come. Thy will be done on earth as it is in heaven. Give us this day our daily bread. And forgive us our trespasses, as we forgive those who trespass against us. And lead us not into temptation. But deliver us from evil. For Thine is the kingdom and the power and the glory forever and ever. Amen.

℄ Then shall the Minister pronounce the Benediction:

THE LORD bless thee and keep thee.

The Lord make His face shine upon thee and be gracious unto thee.

The Lord lift up His countenance upon thee and give thee peace ✠. Amen.

THE ORDER OF

THE CONSECRATION
OF A CIVIL MARRIAGE

✠

❦ If this Order is used in the public church service, it may follow the Offertory in the Order of Morning Service or the Canticle in the Matins and Vespers, and the Lesson should be read at the proper time.

❦ The persons having presented themselves in the church, a suitable Hymn may be sung.

❦ The Minister shall say:

IN THE NAME of the Father and of the Son and of the Holy Ghost.

❦ The Congregation shall say or chant:
Amen.

❦ The Minister shall read Psalm 67 or Psalm 128.

❦ The Congregation shall chant the Gloria Patri.

❦ The Minister, standing before the married pair, who have come to the entrance of the chancel, shall give the Address, or

❦ The Minister shall say:

DEARLY BELOVED: Whereas you have been duly united in wedlock by an official of the civil State and have presented yourselves here to have your marriage consecrated by the Church of Jesus Christ, it behooveth you to hear what the Word of God teacheth concerning marriage.

[53]

The Lord God saith: It is not good that the man should be alone; I will make him an help meet for him.

Our Lord Jesus Christ saith: Have ye not read that He which made them at the beginning, made them male and female, and said, For this cause shall a man leave father and mother, and shall cleave to his wife; and they twain shall be one flesh? Wherefore they are no more twain, but one flesh. What therefore God hath joined together, let not man put asunder.

The Apostle Paul, speaking by the Holy Ghost, saith: Husbands, love your wives, even as Christ also loved the Church and gave Himself for it. So ought men to love their wives as their own bodies. He that loveth his wife loveth himself. For no man ever yet hated his own flesh, but nourisheth and cherisheth it, even as the Lord the Church. Wives, submit yourselves unto your own husbands as unto the Lord. For the husband is the head of the wife, even as Christ is the Head of the Church; and He is the Savior of the body. Therefore as the Church is subject unto Christ, so let the wives be to their own husbands in everything.

And although, by reason of sin, many a cross hath been laid upon this estate, nevertheless our gracious Father in heaven doth not forsake His children in an estate so holy and acceptable to Him, but is ever present with His bountiful blessings.

For thus saith the Lord in the Psalm: Blessed is everyone that feareth the Lord, that walketh in His ways. For thou shalt eat the labor of thine hands. Happy shalt thou be, and it shall be well with thee. Thy wife shall be as a fruitful vine by the sides of thine house; thy children like olive plants round about thy table. Behold, that thus shall the man be blessed that feareth the Lord. The Lord shall bless thee out of Zion; and thou shalt see the good of Jerusalem all the days of thy life. Yea, thou shalt see thy children's children and peace upon Israel.

Thus hath our heavenly Father sanctified the estate of matrimony. He will ever bless therein all who love Him, trust in Him, and live in His fear, for Jesus' sake.

Dearly beloved, as you have united in this holy estate, which consisteth in your mutual consent, sincerely and earnestly given, it behooveth you to declare the same before God and these witnesses.

❧ Then shall the Minister say to the man:

N., Hast thou taken this woman to be thy wedded wife, to live with her after God's ordinance in the holy estate of matrimony, to love her, comfort her, honor her, and keep her in sickness and in health, and, forsaking all others, to keep thee only unto her so long as ye both shall live?

❧ The man shall say:
  I have.

❧ Then shall the Minister say unto the woman:

N., Hast thou taken this man to be thy wedded husband, to live with him after God's ordinance in the holy estate of matrimony, to love him, comfort him, honor and obey him, and keep him in sickness and in health, and, forsaking all others, to keep thee only unto him so long as ye both shall live?

❧ The woman shall say:
  I have.

❧ If the wedding ring be used, the Minister shall now receive it and deliver it to the man to be put on the fourth finger of the woman's left hand.

❡ Then shall the man, facing the woman, say, or if two rings be used, the man and the woman, facing each other, in turn, shall say, after the Minister:

RECEIVE THIS RING / as a pledge and token / of wedded love and faithfulness.

❡ Then shall the Minister say:

MAY THE GIVING and receiving of this ring (these rings) ever be a symbol of the faithful and unselfish community of goods that you as husband and wife, in weal and woe, will cultivate without ceasing, and a reminder of the excellent Christian virtues with which you will adorn your marriage. To this end may God bless you through the heavenly Bridegroom, Jesus Christ, our Lord.

❡ Then shall the Minister say:

JOIN your right hands. What therefore God hath joined together, let not man put asunder.

❡ Then shall they turn to face the altar and kneel, and the Minister shall bless them, saying:

MAY THE ALMIGHTY AND ETERNAL GOD look down from His exalted throne in heaven upon you with His favor and sanctify and bless you with the benediction first spoken to Adam and Eve in Paradise, that you may please Him both in body and soul, and live together in holy love until life's end.

The God of Abraham, the God of Isaac, the God of Jacob, be with you and richly bless you forevermore. Amen.

❡ Then may be sung a Hymn.

❡ Then shall the Minister say or chant:

LET us pray:

Almighty God, our heavenly Father, who hast united this man and this woman in the holy estate of matrimony, grant them the grace to live therein according to Thy holy Word, strengthen them in constant faithfulness and true love toward each other; sustain and defend them amidst all trials and temptations; and help them so to pass through this world in faith towards Thee, in communion with Thy holy Church, and in loving service one of the other, that they may ever enjoy Thy heavenly benediction; through Jesus Christ, Thy Son, our Lord, who liveth and reigneth with Thee and the Holy Ghost, ever one God, world without end.

❡ The Congregation shall say or chant:
Amen.

❡ Then shall all say:
Our Father who art in heaven. Hallowed be Thy name. Thy kingdom come. Thy will be done on earth as it is in heaven. Give us this day our daily bread. And forgive us our trespasses, as we forgive those who trespass against us. And lead us not into temptation. But deliver us from evil. For Thine is the kingdom and the power and the glory forever and ever. Amen.

❡ Then shall the Minister say or chant the Benediction:

THE LORD bless thee and keep thee.

The Lord make His face shine upon thee and be gracious unto thee.

The Lord lift up His countenance upon thee and give thee peace ✠.

❡ Then shall the Congregation say or chant:
Amen.

SILENT PRAYER

THE ORDER FOR

THE ANNIVERSARY
OF A MARRIAGE

✠

❡ If this Order is used in the public church service, it may follow the Offertory in the Order of Morning Service or the Canticle in the Matins and Vespers, and the Lesson should be read at the proper time.

❡ The anniversary couple having presented themselves at the altar, a Hymn of Praise may be sung.

❡ Then shall the Minister say:

OUR HELP is in the name of the Lord, who made heaven and earth.

Beloved in the Lord: These Christian spouses appear this day before the Lord to renew the remembrance of that covenant of matrimony which was made between them ——— years ago, to offer to the Lord the sacrifice of thanksgiving for all the mercies and all the truth which for so many years He hath shown unto them, and to supplicate His gracious aid for the portion that remaineth of their days. Let us pray:

O Thou faithful and merciful God, heavenly Father, who hast instituted the estate of matrimony, hallowed it by the presence of Thy Son at the marriage in Cana of Galilee, and protected and preserved it until this day: we thank Thee for Thy goodness and heartily beseech Thee, Thou wouldst evermore maintain Thine ordinance by Thy gracious and almighty presence, and grant unto these, and all others united in marriage, peace and unity, and comfort and hope in the day of trouble; through Jesus Christ, our Lord. Amen.

❡ Then may another Hymn be sung.

❡ Then shall follow a short Address.

❡ For the Address one of the following texts may be used: Gen. 32:10; 1 Sam. 7:12; 2 Sam. 7:18; Job 10:12; Ps. 9:1-2; Ps. 40:5; Ps. 64: 9-10; Ps. 71:17-18; Ps. 92:13; Ps. 115:13, 15; Ps. 128:5; Prov. 16:16; Prov. 17:6; Is. 46:4; Zech. 8:4; 1 Cor. 15:10.

BELOVED IN THE LORD: Inasmuch as God, of His bountiful goodness, hath permitted you to live together in holy wedlock these —— years, to share with each other both joy and sorrow and to walk together in love and faithfulness that may not be broken so that you are able to celebrate this day of thanksgiving: you heartily desire to commit also the remainder of your days to His gracious care and humbly to implore His blessing. Lift up your hearts, therefore, and offer your thanksgiving unto the Lord and pray:

❡ Now follows the prayer, the celebrating couple kneeling.

LORD GOD, heavenly Father, we give Thee thanks for the fatherly love and grace which Thou hast bestowed upon us, Thine unworthy servants, in such rich measure since the days of our youth and especially during these —— years of holy wedlock. Thou hast accompanied us with loving-kindnesses and tender mercies, visited us with Thy comfort, strengthened us in sorrow and sickness, and hast crowned our life with every blessing. To Thee alone, O most merciful God, belong all honor and praise, for Thou hast helped us to walk in marital love and fidelity without forsaking each other; nor didst Thou forsake us in sickness or health, in weal or woe, in adversity or prosperity, but didst grant us comfort and strength, patience and faithfulness. Be Thou with us in the future, O Lord, until the end of our days. Be Thou our

Guide as Thou hast guided us in the past. Be Thou our Light though the light of our eyes begins to dim. Be Thou our Strength though our strength departs. Be Thou our Support though earthly supports fall. Be Thou our Health in sickness and infirmity. Be Thou our Refuge and our Life in the hour of death. When the days of our, pilgrimage on earth shall cease, graciously bring us to the marriage supper of Thy Son and our Lord Jesus Christ, that we may dwell with Thee and rejoice in Thy joy forever.

¶ Then may the Minister, turning to the kneeling celebrating couple and laying his right hand upon their hands, say:

MAY THE MERCIFUL GOD AND FATHER, who hath hitherto sustained and blessed you by His grace in your wedded life, grant unto you the continuance of His divine protection and blessing and cause your hearts to remain united in faithful love unto the end ✠. Amen.

Peace be with you.

¶ Then shall the Minister, facing the altar, say or chant:

LET us pray:

O almighty God, most merciful Father, we bless and praise Thee for all Thy loving-kindness and tender mercies which, for so many years, Thou hast bestowed upon these Thy servants, providing for them by Thy bounty, defending them by Thy power, and guiding them by Thy mercy. We beseech Thee, let the sacrifice of thanksgiving which they offer to Thee be acceptable in Thy sight, and give ear to their humble requests. During the days which still remain of their pilgrimage on earth, even to their old age, be Thou their Strength and their Deliverer in every infirmity and peril of body and soul.

Let them at all times know the comfort and peace of Thy
Holy Spirit. Be Thou with them, and fulfill in them Thy
promise that the house of the righteous shall stand and the
tabernacle of the upright shall flourish forevermore. And
finally, let them depart this life in joy and peace and with rejoicing meet in Thy heavenly kingdom to laud and praise
Thee and the Son and the Holy Ghost, world without end.
Amen.

❡ Then the Minister, facing the anniversary couple, shall say:

Go Your Way, then, beloved in Christ, whom we have
blessed in the name of the Lord and commended to His gracious
keeping. May your hearts continue to be united in love and
truth and your home to be a dwelling place of the Lord, that,
at the end of your sojourning here on earth, you may together
see God face to face and enjoy that glory which He hath
promised unto all who abide in true faith unto the end. Amen.

❡ Then may another Hymn be sung.

❡ Then shall the Minister say or chant the Benediction.

The Lord bless thee and keep thee.

The Lord make His face shine upon thee and be gracious
unto thee.

The Lord lift up His countenance upon thee and give thee
peace ✠ .

❡ The Congregation shall say or chant:
Amen.

SILENT PRAYER

THE ORDER FOR

THE COMMUNION
OF THE SICK

✠

℄ The Minister may say:

IN THE NAME of the Father and of the Son and of the Holy Ghost. Amen.

℄ Then may the Minister say the following or some other Prayer on behalf of the sick person:

ALMIGHTY AND EVERLASTING GOD, who didst give Thine only Son into death for my sins and through Him didst institute the holy Sacrament of His body and blood for the strengthening of my faith: I call upon Thee in this hour of my sickness as I desire to receive Holy Communion for a comfort in my affliction. Enlighten me by Thy Holy Spirit that I may rightly know and willingly confess my sins. Enable me also with true faith to embrace my only Mediator and Redeemer, Jesus Christ, that I may obtain both pardon and peace and be prepared to partake worthily of Thy Holy Supper to my soul's health. Strengthen me through this salutary gift in faith towards Thee and in fervent love toward all men. Create in me a clean heart, and renew a right spirit within me. Cause me also to recognize in this present visitation Thy fatherly hand, that I may bear my cross in cheerful submission to Thy holy will; and do Thou deal with me according to Thine infinite mercy as Thou alone best knowest, for the sake of Thy dear Son, Jesus Christ, my Lord. Amen.

❡ Then may the Minister read a Psalm (e. g., 6, 25, 32, 38, 42, 51, 71, 77, 130, 143), adding thereto a suitable Exhortation.

❡ The regular form for Confession and Absolution may be used as follows:

O ALMIGHTY GOD, merciful Father, I, a poor, miserable sinner, confess unto Thee all my sins and iniquities, with which I have ever offended Thee and justly deserved Thy temporal and eternal punishment. But I am heartily sorry for them and sincerely repent of them, and I pray Thee, of Thy boundless mercy and for the sake of the holy, innocent, bitter sufferings and death of Thy beloved Son, Jesus Christ, to be gracious and merciful to me, a poor, sinful being. Amen.

Is this thy sincere confession, then declare so by saying, Yes.
Yes.

UPON THIS THY CONFESSION, I, by virtue of my office, as a called and ordained servant of the Word, announce unto thee the grace of God, and in the stead and by the command of my Lord Jesus Christ I forgive thee all thy sins in the name of God the Father, God the Son, and God the Holy Ghost. Amen.

❡ Or the Minister may say:

DOST THOU HUMBLY ACKNOWLEDGE and heartily lament thy sins?
I do.

DOST THOU BELIEVE that God, thy merciful Father, for the sake of Jesus Christ, thy Savior, pardoneth all thine offenses?
I do believe.

ART THOU RESOLVED, if God prolong thy life, to lead the remainder of thy life in His fear and to His glory?
I am resolved.

Be It unto Thee according to thy faith. And I, by the command of our Lord Jesus Christ, upon this thy confession, forgive thee all thy sins in the name of the Father and of the Son and of the Holy Ghost. Amen.

Peace be with thee ✠.

⁋ Then shall the Minister and the sick person with him say

THE APOSTLES' CREED

I Believe in God the Father Almighty, Maker of heaven and earth.

And in Jesus Christ, His only Son, our Lord; Who was conceived by the Holy Ghost, Born of the Virgin Mary; Suffered under Pontius Pilate, Was crucified, dead, and buried; He descended into hell; The third day He rose again from the dead; He ascended into heaven And sitteth on the right hand of God the Father Almighty; From thence He shall come to judge the quick and the dead.

I believe in the Holy Ghost; The holy Christian Church, the communion of saints; The forgiveness of sins; The resurrection of the body; And the life everlasting. Amen.

Let us pray:

Our Father who art in heaven. Hallowed be Thy name. Thy kingdom come. Thy will be done on earth as it is in heaven. Give us this day our daily bread. And forgive us our trespasses, as we forgive those who trespass against us. And lead us not into temptation. But deliver us from evil. For Thine is the kingdom and the power and the glory forever and ever. Amen.

Our Lord Jesus Christ, the same night in which He was

betrayed, took bread; and when He had given thanks, He brake it and gave it to His disciples, saying, Take, eat; this is My body ✠, which is given for you. This do in remembrance of Me.

After the same manner also He took the cup when He had supped, and when He had given thanks, He gave it to them, saying, Drink ye all of it; this cup is the new testament in My blood ✠, which is shed for you for the remission of sins. This do, as oft as ye drink it, in remembrance of Me.

Take, eat; this is the true body of our Lord and Savior Jesus Christ, given into death for thy sins. May this strengthen and preserve thee in the true faith unto life everlasting!

Take, drink; this is the true blood of our Lord and Savior Jesus Christ, shed for the remission of thy sins. May this strengthen and preserve thee in the true faith unto life everlasting! Amen.

❡ A Psalm (e. g., 23, 103, 111, 118) may be read, followed by the Thanksgiving.

PSALM 23

THE LORD is my Shepherd; I shall not want. He maketh me to lie down in green pastures; He leadeth me beside the still waters.

He restoreth my soul; He leadeth me in the paths of righteousness for His name's sake.

Yea, though I walk through the valley of the shadow of death, I will fear no evil; for Thou art with me; Thy rod and Thy staff, they comfort me.

Thou preparest a table before me in the presence of mine enemies; Thou anointest my head with oil; my cup runneth .over.

Surely, goodness and mercy shall follow me all the days of my life; and I will dwell in the house of the Lord forever.

O LORD JESUS, my Savior and only Refuge, I give Thee hearty thanks that Thou hast so graciously refreshed me with Thy sacred body and blood. Uphold me with Thy grace, and strengthen me by Thy power. Into Thy hands I commit my body and soul, whether for life or for death. Grant that, when my last hour shall come, I may fall asleep in firm faith in Thee and Thy sacred blood, O Thou, who livest and reignest. world without end. Amen.

❡ Or:

I THANK THEE, Almighty God, that Thou hast refreshed me with this salutary gift; and I beseech Thee, of Thy mercy, to strengthen me through the same in faith toward Thee, in love toward all mankind, in patience under trials, and in the blessed hope of everlasting life; through Jesus Christ, Thy Son, our Lord, who liveth and reigneth with Thee and the Holy Ghost, ever one God, world without end. Amen.

❡ Or:

ALMIGHTY GOD, heavenly Father, I heartily thank Thee that Thou hast refreshed me with the body and blood of Thy dear Son Jesus Christ, and I beseech Thee, cause this heavenly food so to strengthen my faith that I may bear my cross with Christian patience and trust until it shall please Thee to grant me deliverance; through Jesus Christ, Thy Son, our Lord. Amen.

THE LORD bless thee and keep thee.

The Lord make His face shine upon thee and be gracious unto thee.

The Lord lift up His countenance upon thee and give thee peace ✠. Amen.

THE ORDER FOR

THE BURIAL OF THE DEAD

✠

AT THE HOUSE OR AT THE FUNERAL HOME

❡ It is customary to hold a brief service at the house before going to the church or to the grave.

❡ This Order is intended only for the burial of those who depart this life in the Christian faith.

❡ When the entire service is held in a funeral home, the following Order may also be used.

❡ A Hymn may be sung.

❡ The Minister may use one or more of the following Versicles:

GRACE TO YOU and peace from God, our Father, and the Lord Jesus Christ.

Unto our God, who alone hath immortality, be honor and power both now and forevermore.

Our help is in the name of the Lord, who made heaven and earth.

Like as a father pitieth his children, so the Lord pitieth them that fear Him. For He knoweth our frame; He remembereth that we are dust.

Blessed be God, even the Father of our Lord Jesus Christ, the Father of mercies and the God of all comfort, who comforteth us in all our tribulation, that we may be able to comfort them which are in any trouble, by the comfort wherewith we ourselves are comforted of God.

[67]

❡ If desired. an Address may be given instead of the following Exhortation.

BELOVED IN THE LORD: Forasmuch as it hath pleased Almighty God in His good providence to call this *brother* out of this present life, it becometh us, before committing *his* body to the earth, to hear in our bereavement the admonition and comfort of God's holy Word.

Thus saith the Lord: Dust thou art, and unto dust shalt thou return. By one man sin entered into the world and death by sin; and so death passed upon all men, for that all have sinned. There is no respect of persons; we die the common death of all men; for the wages of sin is death. May we, then, with a deep sense of our sinfulness humble ourselves under the mighty hand of God, before whom we are dust, and earnestly ponder the rapid flight of our days. Man that is born of a woman is of few days and full of trouble. He cometh forth like a flower, and is cut down; he fleeth also as a shadow. and continueth not. We cannot but say with David: Behold, Thou hast made my days as an handbreadth; and mine age is as nothing before Thee. Verily, every man at his best state is altogether vanity. But blessed be God, even the Father of our Lord Jesus Christ, the Father of mercies and the God of all comfort, who hath loved us and hath given us everlasting consolation and good hope through grace, and hath begotten us again unto a lively hope by the resurrection of Jesus Christ from the dead.

For as in Adam all die, even so in Christ shall all be made alive. Being delivered for our offenses, He was raised again for our justification and hath brought life and immortality to light through the Gospel. He is the First Fruits of them that sleep, and saith: I am the Resurrection and the Life; he that believeth in Me. though he were dead, yet shall he live; and whosoever liveth and believeth in Me shall never die. Therefore in life and in death He is our Comfort; for through Him the death of His own is swallowed up in victory, and by faith in Him we have part in His gracious promise: This corruptible must put on incorruption, and this mortal must put on immortality. It is sown in weakness, it is raised in power; it is sown in dishonor, it is raised in glory. And as we have borne the image of the earthy, we shall also bear the image of the heavenly, the image of our Lord Jesus Christ, who shall change our vile body that it may be fashioned like unto His glorious body.

Therefore we sorrow not, even as others that have no hope, but lift up our heads, knowing that our Redeemer liveth and that the souls of the righteous are in the hand of God, where no torment shall touch them. Blessed are the dead which die in the Lord from henceforth; yea, saith the Spirit, that they may rest from their labors; and their works do follow them.

Every man that hath this hope in Him purifieth himself, even as Christ is pure. For we must all appear before the judgment seat of Christ, that everyone may receive the things done in his body according to that he hath done, whether it be good or bad. Therefore, beloved, let us escape the corruption that is in the world through lust, and seek now, in the day of salvation, the one thing needful, which shall not be taken away from us. Let us fight the good fight of faith and lay hold on eternal life, whereunto we are also called. May we be found in constant readiness for the final summons, ever waiting for our Lord and purifying our souls in obeying the truth through His Spirit, that, through His power resting upon us, we may overcome the world and be counted worthy at last to reign with Him eternally in heaven.

❡ Then shall a Scripture Lesson be read, e. g.:

PSALM 90

LORD, Thou hast been our Dwelling Place in all generations.

Before the mountains were brought forth or ever Thou hadst formed the earth and the world, even from everlasting to everlasting, Thou art God.

Thou turnest man to destruction and sayest, Return, ye children of men.

For a thousand years in Thy sight are but as yesterday when it is past and as a watch in the night.

Thou carriest them away as with a flood; they are as a sleep; in the morning they are like grass which groweth up.

In the morning it flourisheth and groweth up; in the evening it is cut down and withereth.

For we are consumed by Thine anger, and by Thy wrath are we troubled.

Thou hast set our iniquities before Thee, our secret sins in the light of Thy countenance.

For all our days are passed away in Thy wrath; we spend our years as a tale that is told.

The days of our years are threescore years and ten; and if by reason of strength they be fourscore years, yet is their strength labor and sorrow, for it is soon cut off, and we fly away.

Who knoweth the power of Thine anger? Even according to Thy fear, so is Thy wrath.

So teach us to number our days, that we may apply our hearts unto wisdom.

Return, O Lord, how long? And let it repent Thee concerning Thy servants.

Oh, satisfy us early with Thy mercy; that we may rejoice and be glad all our days.

Make us glad according to the days wherein Thou hast afflicted us and the years wherein we have seen evil.

Let Thy work appear unto Thy servants, and Thy glory unto their children.

And let the beauty of the Lord our God be upon us; and establish Thou the work of our hands upon us; yea, the work of our hands establish Thou it.

JOHN 5:24

VERILY, verily, I say unto you, He that heareth My Word and believeth on Him that sent Me hath everlasting life and shall not come into condemnation, but is passed from death unto life.

JOHN 10:27-29

MY SHEEP hear My voice, and I know them, and they follow Me;

And I give unto them eternal life; and they shall never perish, neither shall any man pluck them out of My hand.

My Father, which gave them Me, is greater than all; and no man is able to pluck them out of My Father's hand.

PSALM 130

OUT OF THE DEPTHS have I cried unto Thee, O Lord.

Lord, hear my voice; let Thine ears be attentive to the voice of my supplications.

If Thou, Lord, shouldest mark iniquities, O Lord, who shall stand?

But there is forgiveness with Thee, that Thou mayest be feared.

I wait for the Lord, my soul doth wait, and in His Word do I hope.

My soul waiteth for the Lord more than they that watch for the morning; I say, more than they that watch for the morning.

Let Israel hope in the Lord, for with the Lord there is mercy, and with Him is plenteous redemption.

And He shall redeem Israel from all his iniquities.

PSALM 23

THE LORD is my Shepherd; I shall not want.

He maketh me to lie down in green pastures; He leadeth me beside the still waters.

He restoreth my soul; He leadeth me in the paths of righteousness for His name's sake.

Yea, though I walk through the valley of the shadow of death, I will fear no evil; for Thou art with me; Thy rod and Thy staff, they comfort me.

Thou preparest a table before me in the presence of mine enemies; Thou anointest my head with oil; my cup runneth over.

Surely, goodness and mercy shall follow me all the days of my life; and I will dwell in the house of the Lord forever.

1 THESS. 4:13-18

BUT I WOULD NOT HAVE you to be ignorant, brethren, concerning them which are asleep, that ye sorrow not, even as others which have no hope. For if we believe that Jesus died and rose again, even so them also which sleep in Jesus will God bring with Him. For this we say unto you by the word of the Lord that we which are alive and remain unto the coming of the Lord shall not prevent them which are asleep.

For the Lord Himself shall descend from heaven with a shout, with the voice of the archangel, and with the trump of God; and the dead in Christ shall rise first.   Then we which are alive and remain shall be caught up together with them in the clouds to meet the Lord in the air; and so shall we ever be with the Lord.   Wherefore comfort one another with these words.

JOHN 14:1-6

LET NOT YOUR HEART be troubled.   Ye believe in God, believe also in Me.   In My Father's house are many mansions; if it were not so, I would have told you.   I go to prepare a place for you.   And if I go and prepare a place for you, I will come again and receive you unto Myself, that, where I am, there ye may be also.   And whither I go ye know, and the way ye know.   Thomas saith unto Him: Lord, we know not whither Thou goest; and how can we know the way?   Jesus saith unto him: I am the Way, the Truth, and the Life: no man cometh unto the Father but by Me.

AT THE DEATH OF A CHILD

JOB 14:1-2

MAN THAT IS BORN of a woman is of few days and full of trouble.   He cometh forth like a flower, and is cut down; he fleeth also as a shadow, and continueth not.

JOB 5:6-7

ALTHOUGH affliction cometh not forth of the dust, neither doth trouble spring out of the ground; yet man is born unto trouble, as the sparks fly upward.

JOB 1:21

THE LORD gave, and the Lord hath taken away; blessed be the name of the Lord.

IS. 40:11

HE SHALL FEED His flock like a shepherd; He shall gather the lambs with His arm and carry them in His bosom and shall gently lead those that are with young.

JER. 31:15-17

THUS SAITH THE LORD: A voice was heard in Ramah, lamentation and bitter weeping; Rachel, weeping for her children, refused to be comforted for her children, because they were not. Thus saith the Lord: Refrain thy voice from weeping and thine eyes from tears; for thy work shall be rewarded, saith the Lord; and they shall come again from the land of the enemy. And there is hope in thine end, saith the Lord, that thy children shall come again to their own border.

MARK 10:13-16

AND THEY BROUGHT young children to Jesus, that He should touch them; and His disciples rebuked those that brought them. But when Jesus saw it, He was much displeased and said unto them: Suffer the little children to come unto Me, and forbid them not, for of such is the Kingdom of God. Verily, I say unto you: Whosoever shall not receive the Kingdom of God as a little child, he shall not enter therein. And He took them up in His arms, put His hands upon them, and blessed them.

AT THE DEATH OF A YOUNG PERSON

PSALM 103:15-16

AS FOR MAN, his days are as grass; as a flower of the field, so he flourisheth. For the wind passeth over it, and it is gone, and the place thereof shall know it no more.

PSALM 39:5

Behold, Thou hast made my days as an handbreadth, and mine age is as nothing before Thee.   Verily, every man at his best state is altogether vanity

JOB 9:25-26

Now My Days are swifter than a post; they flee away, they see no good.   They are passed away as the swift ships, as the eagle that hasteth to the prey.

PROV. 27:1

Boast Not Thyself of tomorrow, for thou knowest not what a day may bring forth.

ECCL. 11:7-10

Truly, the light is sweet, and a pleasant thing it is for the eyes to behold the sun; but if a man live many years and rejoice in them all, yet let him remember the days of darkness, for they shall be many.   All that cometh is vanity.   Rejoice, O young man, in thy youth, and let thy heart cheer thee in the days of thy youth, and walk in the ways of thine heart and in the sight of thine eyes; but know thou that for all these things God will bring thee into judgment.   Therefore remove sorrow from thy heart, and put away evil from thy flesh; for childhood and youth are vanity.

JAMES 4:14

For What is your life?   It is even a vapor that appeareth for a little time and then vanisheth away.

LUKE 7:11-17

And It Came to Pass the day after, that He went into a city called Nain; and many of His disciples went with Him and much people.   Now, when He came nigh to the gate of

the city, behold, there was a dead man carried out, the only
son of his mother, and she was a widow; and much people
of the city was with her.   And when the Lord saw her, He
had compassion on her and said unto her: Weep not.   And
He came and touched the bier; and they that bare him stood
still.   And He said. Young man, I say unto thee, Arise.   And
he that was dead sat up and began to speak.   And He delivered him to his mother.   And there came a fear on all; and
they glorified God, saying, That a great prophet is risen up
among us; and, That God hath visited His people.   And this
rumor of Him went forth throughout all Judea and throughout all the region round about.

MATT. 9:18-19, 23-26

WHILE HE SPAKE these things unto them, behold, there came
a certain ruler and worshiped Him, saying: My daughter is
even now dead; but come, and lay Thy hand upon her, and
she shall live.   And Jesus arose and followed him, and so
did His disciples.

And when Jesus came into the ruler's house and saw the
minstrels and the people making a noise, He said unto them:
Give place, for the maid is not dead, but sleepeth.   And they
laughed Him to scorn.   But when the people were put forth,
He went in and took her by the hand, and the maid arose.
And the fame hereof went abroad into all that land.

MATT. 25:1-13

THEN shall the kingdom of heaven be likened unto ten virgins
which took their lamps and went forth to meet the bridegroom.   And five of them were wise, and five were foolish.
They that were foolish took their lamps and took no oil with
them; but the wise took oil in their vessels with their lamps.

While the bridegroom tarried, they all slumbered and slept. And at midnight there was a cry made: Behold, the bridegroom cometh; go ye out to meet him! Then all those virgins arose and trimmed their lamps. And the foolish said unto the wise, Give us of your oil; for our lamps are gone out. But the wise answered, saying: Not so, lest there be not enough for us and you; but go ye rather to them that sell, and buy for yourselves. And while they went to buy, the bridegroom came; and they that were ready went in with him to the marriage. And the door was shut. Afterward came also the other virgins, saying, Lord, Lord, open to us! But he answered and said: Verily, I say unto you, I know you not. Watch therefore; for ye know neither the day nor the hour wherein the Son of Man cometh.

AT THE DEATH OF THE AGED

PSALM 92:12-15

THE RIGHTEOUS shall flourish like the palm tree; he shall grow like a cedar in Lebanon. Those that be planted in the house of the Lord shall flourish in the courts of our God. They shall still bring forth fruit in old age; they shall be fat and flourishing; to show that the Lord is upright. He is my Rock, and there is no unrighteousness in Him.

PROV. 16:31

THE HOARY HEAD is a crown of glory if it be found in the way of righteousness.

IS. 46:4

AND EVEN TO YOUR OLD AGE I am He, and even to hoar hairs will I carry you. I have made, and I will bear; even I will carry and will deliver you.

2 TIM. 4:6-8

FOR I AM NOW READY to be offered, and the time of my departure is at hand. I have fought a good fight, I have finished my course, I have kept the faith; henceforth there is laid up for me a crown of righteousness, which the Lord, the righteous Judge, shall give me at that day; and not to me only, but unto all them that love His appearing.

PHIL. 3:20-21

FOR OUR CONVERSATION is in heaven, from whence also we look for the Savior, the Lord Jesus Christ, who shall change our vile body that it may be fashioned like unto His glorious body, according to the working whereby He is able even to subdue all things unto Himself.

The Death of a Child: 2 Sam. 12:15-23; 1 Kings 17:17-24; 2 Kings 4: 18-26; Jer. 31:15-17; Mark 10:13-16.

The Death of a Young Person: Eccl. 11:7-10; Eccl. 12:1-8; Is. 40:30-31; Mark 5:35-43; Luke 7:11-17.

The Death of a Woman: Luke 2:36-38; Acts 9:36-42.

The Death of the Aged: Job 5:17-26; Ps. 71:7-21; Luke 2:25-32; 2 Tim. 4:6-8.

Mortality: Job 14:1-15; Ps. 39:4-13; Is. 40:6-10; Num. 21:6-9, with John 3:14-15; Rom. 8:31-39; James 4:13-15.

Bereavement: Ps. 88:1-18; Ps. 130:1-8; Ps. 143:1-12; Eccl. 7:1-4; Is. 54: 7-13.

Comfort: Ps. 25:1-22; Psalm 46; Ps. 61:1-4; Ps. 103:1-22; Lam. 3: 22-23; John 10:7-16; John 14:1-6.

Hope: Job 19:25-27; Psalm 23; Ps. 42:5-11; 1 Pet. 1:3-9.

Exhortations: Matt. 24:36-47; Matt. 25:1-13; Mark 13:32-37; Luke 12: 35-48; 1 Cor. 7:29-31; Eph. 5:15-21; Eph. 6:10-18; 1 Thess. 5:1-11; 2 Pet. 3:8-14.

Victory: Ps. 31:7-24; Rom. 8:16-25, 31-39; 1 Cor. 15:50-58; Rev. 22: 12-14.

Resurrection: Matt. 28:1-10; Mark 12:26-27; John 5:19-29; John 11: 1-44; 1 Cor. 15:20-28, 35-49; 2 Cor. 4:7-18; Phil. 3:8-11; Col. 3:1-4; 1 Thess. 4:13-18.

Heaven: Matt. 25:34-40; 2 Cor. 5:1-10; Rev. 7:9-17; Rev. 14:13; Rev. 19:5-9; Rev. 21:1-5, 10-13, 22-27; Rev. 22:1-6.

❦ Then shall the Minister say:

LET us pray:

Almighty and most merciful God, who hast appointed us to endure sufferings and death with our Lord Jesus Christ before we enter with Him into glory, grant us grace at all times to submit ourselves to Thy holy will, to continue steadfast in the true faith unto the end, and to find peace and joy in the blessed hope of the resurrection of the dead and of the glory of the world to come; through our Lord Jesus Christ. Amen.

❦ For other suitable Prayers see page 82 and following pages.

THE LORD'S PRAYER

OUR FATHER who art in heaven. Hallowed be Thy name. Thy kingdom come. Thy will be done on earth as it is in heaven. Give us this day our daily bread. And forgive us our trespasses, as we forgive those who trespass against us. And lead us not into temptation. But deliver us from evil. For Thine is the kingdom and the power and the glory forever and ever. Amen.

THE BENEDICTION

THE GRACE of our Lord Jesus Christ ✠ and the love of God and the communion of the Holy Ghost be with you all. Amen.

SILENT PRAYER

AT THE CHURCH

❡ It is not in the best Christian tradition to eulogize the departed;
or to have the funeral service interrupted by the exercises of any secular
organization.

❡ As the Minister, preceding the funeral procession, enters the sanctuary
and walks to the altar, he may read aloud the following Sentences, continuing at the altar until the mourners are in their pews.   Or the Minister
may read these Sentences from the chancel

MAN THAT IS BORN of a woman is of few days and full of
trouble.   He cometh forth like a flower, and is cut down;
he fleeth also as a shadow, and continueth not.   Behold, Thou
hast made my days as an handbreadth;   and mine age is as
nothing before Thee.   Verily, every man at his best state is
altogether vanity.

Thus saith the Lord: Dust thou art, and unto dust shalt
thou return.   By one man sin entered into the world and death
by sin; and so death passed upon all men, for that all have
sinned.

Every man that hath this hope in Him purifieth himself,
even as Christ is pure.   For we must all appear before the
judgment seat of Christ, that everyone may receive the things
done in his body, according to that he hath done, whether it
be good or bad.   Therefore, beloved, let us escape the corruption that is in the world through lust, and seek now, in the
day of salvation, the one thing needful, which shall not be
taken away from us.   Let us fight the good fight of faith, and
lay hold on eternal life, whereunto we are also called.   May
we be found in constant readiness for the final summons, ever
waiting for our Lord and purifying our souls in obeying the
truth through His Spirit, that, through His power resting
upon us, we may overcome the world and be counted worthy
at last to reign with Him eternally in heaven.

Blessed be God, even the Father of our Lord Jesus Christ, the Father of mercies and the God of all comfort, who hath loved us, and hath given us everlasting consolation and good hope through grace, and hath begotten us again unto a lively hope by the resurrection of Jesus Christ from the dead.

For as in Adam all die, even so in Christ shall all be made alive. Being delivered for our offenses, He was raised again for our justification, and hath brought life and immortality to light through the Gospel.

He is the First Fruits of them that sleep, and saith: I am the Resurrection and the Life; he that believeth in Me, though he were dead, yet shall he live; and whosoever liveth and believeth in Me shall never die.

This corruptible must put on incorruption, and this mortal must put on immortality. It is sown in weakness, it is raised in power; it is sown in dishonor, it is raised in glory. And as we have borne the image of the earthy, we shall also bear the image of the heavenly, the image of our Lord Jesus Christ, who shall change our vile body, that it may be fashioned like unto His glorious body.

I heard a voice from heaven saying, Write, Blessed are the dead which die in the Lord from henceforth; yea, saith the Spirit, that they may rest from their labors; and their works do follow them.

℃ The Service may begin with a Hymn.

℃ Then shall the Minister say or chant:

IN THE NAME of the Father and of the Son and of the Holy Ghost.

℃ The Congregation shall say or chant:
Amen.

❡ Then shall be said

THE PSALM

(Psalm 23, Psalm 90, or Psalm 130.   See pages 72, 70, 71)

❡ Then shall be read

THE LESSON

(For appropriate Lessons see pages 70—79)

❡ Then may a Hymn be sung.

❡ Then may follow a Sermon or an Address.

❡ Then may be sung a Hymn, or a Canticle may be sung by the Choir.

❡ Then may messages of condolence be read, or, if customary, the obituary may be read.   Then the following Prayer may be said:

O GOD THE FATHER in heaven, have mercy upon us.

O God the Son, Redeemer of the world, have mercy upon us.

O God the Holy Ghost, have mercy upon us, and grant us Thy peace.

❡ Then may the Minister say one or more of the following Prayers.

1

ALMIGHTY GOD, with whom do live the spirits of those who depart hence in the Lord and with whom the souls of the faithful, after they are delivered from the burden of the flesh, are in joy and happiness, we give Thee hearty thanks for Thy loving-kindness to all those Thy servants who, having finished their course in faith, do now rest from their labors.   And we beseech Thee that we, with all those who are departed in the true faith of Thy holy name, may have our perfect consummation and bliss, both in body and soul, in Thy eternal and everlasting glory; through Jesus Christ, our Lord.   Amen.

2

O LORD, ALMIGHTY AND MERCIFUL GOD, who through death callest us out of this wicked world, that we may not perish through continued sinning, but attain life and glory everlasting, we beseech Thee, fill our hearts with a deep sense of Thy mercy, that we may look·forward with rejoicing to our departure and willingly obey the summons to enter into Thy kingdom; through Jesus Christ, Thy Son, our Lord. Amen.

3

O ALMIGHTY, EVERLASTING GOD AND FATHER, we thank Thee that Thou hast given Thine only-begotten Son Jesus Christ into death for us and through His triumphant resurrection hast given us assurance of eternal life, and we beseech Thee, comfort and raise us up with this assurance, and at last let us come unto eternal rest with Thee; through Jesus Christ, our Lord. Amen.

4

O THOU EVER-BLESSED MEDIATOR, who wast dead, but livest forever, of whom the whole family in heaven and earth is named, and who hast knit all Thy saints in one communion unto life eternal in that mystical body of which Thou art the glorious and everliving Head, grant us grace so to follow Thy blessed saints who have gone before us, in the faith and fellowship of Thy holy Church, that we may come to those unspeakable joys which Thou hast prepared for all that love Thee, from the foundation of the world. Amen.

5

O HOLY AND EVER-BLESSED SPIRIT, who art one with the Father and the Son and who dwellest in all Thy saints to comfort and quicken them, do Thou, we beseech Thee, comfort us in the prospect of death with the hope of the resurrection of the just, and abide in us, that we may ever walk in Thy truth and in the end be found worthy of everlasting life; through Jesus Christ, our Lord. Amen.

6

O HOLY AND ADORABLE TRINITY, Father, Son, and Holy Ghost, Creator, Redeemer, and Sanctifier of our bodies and souls, we humbly confess our sins, and acknowledge them as the cause of our misery and death, and that on account of our sins Thou art justly displeased. Yet, through infinite mercy in Jesus Christ, we implore Thee, blot out our transgressions, wash us from our iniquity, and cleanse us from our sin. O Lord God most holy, O Lord God most mighty, O holy and most merciful Savior, deliver us not into the bitter pains of eternal death. Amen.

7

THOU KNOWEST, Lord, the secrets of our hearts, shut not Thy merciful ears to our prayer, but spare us, Lord most holy, O God most mighty, O holy and merciful Savior. Thou most worthy Judge eternal, suffer us not, at our last hour, for any pains of death, to fall from Thee. But keep us in everlasting fellowship with the Church Triumphant, and let us rest together in Thy presence from our labors; through Jesus Christ, our Lord, who liveth and reigneth with Thee and the Holy Ghost, ever one God, world without end. Amen.

AT THE DEATH OF A CHILD

1

O LORD, almighty, heavenly Father, who art a God of all comfort and dost bid us mourn with the afflicted, we beseech Thee, Thou wouldst with Thy gracious Spirit comfort our *brother* and *sister,* who are mourning the loss of *their* beloved child. Enable *them* in steadfast faith and confident hope·to look for the blessed day of our final redemption, when all who believe in Thee shall meet again in heavenly joy and glory; through Jesus Christ, our Lord. Amen.

2

ALMIGHTY GOD, heavenly Father, who in Thy wise and gracious providence hast called out of this world the soul of this dear *child,* we thank Thee for Thy mercy in receiving *him* as Thine own in Holy Baptism and regenerating *him* unto the inheritance of Thine eternal kingdom. And we beseech Thee, send forth the consolations of Thy holy Word into the hearts that mourn over *his* early death. Give to the afflicted parents a meek submission to Thy fatherly chastenings, that with childlike faith they may praise Thine unsearchable ways. Thou hast cut down the flower in tender bud; help them also to see Thy gracious hand in what they suffer and to realize that what has faded from them here still blooms immortal in the heavens, and that they shall behold their child again in the joy of everlasting life. Let Thy grace abound in them, comforting them in their bereavement, lest they sorrow beyond what is meet and right. Graciously turn Thou this dispensation to their spiritual good, that they may be drawn into still closer communion with Thee and be the better fitted for a devoted life and a glorious immortality. Grant unto us all, while we sojourn here on earth, the aid of Thy Holy Spirit, that we may continue steadfast in faith and in Thy fear, and finally appear in Thy presence with exceeding joy; for the sake of our Lord and Savior Jesus Christ. Amen.

AT THE DEATH OF AN ADULT

1

ALMIGHTY GOD, heavenly Father, we thank and praise Thee
that Thou hast called this our *brother* to the knowledge of
Thy dear Son, kept *him* in the true faith, and granted *him*
a blessed end; and we beseech Thee, help us by Thy Holy
Spirit rightly to know and lament our sins and to be so
strengthened in our faith in Christ that in all things we may
grow up into Him who is our Head, evermore praising Thee
in newness of life and cheerfully awaiting that hope and
glorious appearing of the great God and our Savior Jesus
Christ, who liveth and reigneth with Thee and the Holy
Ghost, world without end. Amen.

2

O MOST MERCIFUL GOD, Father of our Lord Jesus Christ,
under the shadow of Thy sore judgments we come to Thee
as our only Helper. Thou art the Lord, and beside Thee
there is none other. Thou art a very present Help in trouble.
Thou hast entered this house with Thy chastenings and hast
here caused Thy sovereign power to be felt. Oh, be Thou
nigh, in Thy tender compassion, with the comforts of the
Holy Spirit. Bless these Thy sorrowing servants with the
consolation of Thy grace, which alone can afford them help.
Take them into Thy gracious keeping, and fill their bleeding
hearts with the soothing balm of Thy love. Let there be
light in the midst of this dark night of grief. Deliver us all,
O God, from the bondage of our sins, that we may be free
from the fear of death and be ready at Thy call to depart
hence and be at peace. Whether we live, may we live unto
the Lord, or whether we die, may we die unto the Lord. And

so unite us with Christ Jesus, and work in us by the sanctifying influences of the Holy Ghost, that, whether living or dying, we may be the Lord's. Amen.

3

O MERCIFUL GOD, heavenly Father, forasmuch as it hath pleased Thee to summon another member of our congregation out of this present life and again to remind us that our life appeareth only for a little time; we beseech Thee, gird us with the power of Thy Holy Spirit, that, amidst the vanities of this world, we may fight a good fight and keep the faith, thus finishing the course of our pilgrimage on earth in all holy obedience, in constant watchfulness and prayer, lest death come upon us unawares and find us unprepared. Comfort us in the hour of death with the bitter sufferings and death of Thy Son, who was delivered for our offenses and raised again for our justification, that we may depart this life at peace with Thee and receive the crown of righteousness; through Thy dear Son, our Lord and Redeemer, Jesus Christ. Amen.

4

ALMIGHTY, ETERNAL GOD, Thy years are throughout all generations; we, however, shall perish in time; for all flesh is as grass and all the glory of man as the flower of grass. The grass withereth, and the flower thereof falleth away. Make us to know our end and the measure of our days what it is, that we may know how frail we are, daily trim our lamps, and wait by faith for a blessed end. Suffer not the thoughts and the sting of death to make us afraid, but let us at all times look unto our Lord Jesus Christ, who hath abolished death and hath brought life and immortality to light through the Gospel. Keep us by Thy Spirit in faith and good conscience; for he that soweth to his flesh shall of the flesh reap corruption; but he that soweth to the Spirit shall of the Spirit reap life everlasting. At the removal of our loved ones who die in the Lord, enable us to understand that they are blessed from henceforth and go to Thee, where there shall be neither sorrow nor crying, neither any more pain, and where Thou wilt wipe away all tears from their eyes. O Lord God, Thou beholdest all our affliction and pain, the poor commit themselves unto Thee, Thou art the Helper of the widows and the fatherless. Be pleased to appear with Thy strong comfort to all that are afflicted and distressed, and finally present them, together with the dead for whom they mourn, before Thy presence with exceeding joy. When our last hour shall come, let us, Thy servants, depart in peace. Preserve us from a sudden, evil death; and, being full of faith and rich in the fruits of righteousness, let us commit our spirit into Thy hands and thus finish our course and lay hold on eternal life. Amen.

5

O LORD GOD, who hast called this our departed *brother* hence in the noontide of *his* life and labors, we humble ourselves under Thy holy will and reverence Thy ways, although Thy judgments are unsearchable and Thy ways past finding out. For Thou thinkest towards us thoughts of peace and not of evil, and all things work together for good to them that love Thee. We thank Thee that of Thy fatherly love Thou didst bestow upon this our *brother* Thy merciful guidance, Thy faithful protection, and Thy constant blessing in body and soul, even unto the end. We beseech Thee to comfort with Thy holy Word the hearts of those who are bowed down by *his* death and to strengthen them by the assurance that even through crosses and trials Thou wouldst bless them and dost chasten Thy children, not to destroy them, but that they may live. Enable us all to lay to heart that our sojourning

on earth is but for a little time, that we may diligently ponder
in this our day the things which belong unto our peace.
Sanctify us through Thy truth, and purify our hearts by
faith, that we may not love the fleeting pleasures of this world,
but, ordering our lives agreeably to Thy will, seek those things
that are above and at the last appear before Thy presence in
peace and joy. Grant all this, we pray Thee, for the sake of
Jesus Christ, Thy dear Son. Amen.

6

WE THANK THEE, Lord Jesus Christ, that Thou hast taken
our *brother* away from distress and brought *him* into eternal
rest. O dear Savior, we say with Job: The Lord gave, and
the Lord hath taken away; blessed be the name of the Lord;
and with the people in the Gospel: He hath done all things
well. Enable us to comfort ourselves with the consideration
that we have not lost *him*, but have only sent *him* before,
nowise doubting that on the Last Day Thou wilt raise up
with power and great glory the dead body here lying before
us in weakness and that we shall find one another again with
Thee in eternal life. May it also please Thee to grant us the
grace of Thy Holy Spirit that at this burial we may call to
mind how soon it is all over with men and be found in constant and never-failing Christian readiness to follow Thee,
when the hour is at hand, through the dark valley of death
into Thy kingdom with exceeding joy; O Thou, who, with
the Father and the Holy Ghost, livest and reignest, world
without end. Amen.

7

(At the Death of a Husband and Father)

ALMIGHTY AND MOST MERCIFUL GOD, in whose hands are
all the children of men, teach us to number our days, that we
may apply our hearts unto wisdom. Give us grace to live by

faith in Thy dear Son Jesus Christ and to do what our hands find to do, that, when He who is our Life shall appear, we also may appear with Him in glory. To Thy fatherly goodness do we commend those whom Thou hast afflicted by this dispensation of Thy providence. Let the pains of their bereavement be softened by the assurances of Thy holy Word. Cause the fruits of this their sore chastenings to be righteousness and peace. Let the removal of their beloved and cherished one serve to direct their affections heavenward, that they may seek those things which are above, where Christ sitteth. Be Thou a Father of the fatherless and a Helper of the widow. Remind them of Thy gracious covenant of old, and let not Thy mercy depart from them. Fulfill unto them Thy blessed promise that all things shall work together for good to them that love Thee. May they not sorrow as those who have no hope, but have abundant consolations for all their griefs and a far more exceeding and eternal weight of glory for all their sufferings in this life. These blessings, and all others which may be needful for us and for all men, we humbly ask in the name and for the sake of our blessed Lord and Savior Jesus Christ. Amen.

8

(At the Death of a Wife and Mother)

ETERNAL GOD, merciful Father, look graciously upon us, who sorrow at the loss of a Christian sister, a beloved wife and mother. Teach us, O Father, to know that Thy thoughts are higher than our thoughts and Thy ways higher than our ways, that we may submit ourselves to Thy fatherly will and say: Thou doest all things well. Help us call to mind the manifold mercies which from her youth Thou hast bestowed upon our departed sister in receiving her by Holy Baptism as Thine own dear child, comforting her with the forgiveness of sins in Christ Jesus, guiding her feet into the paths of uprightness, and removing her at length from all earthly sorrow into the unending joy of heaven. Let us not mourn as those who have no hope, for blessed indeed are the dead that die in the Lord from henceforth. Enable us to comfort ourselves with the assurance that Thou wilt raise up with power and glory the body here sown in weakness and that we shall behold her again with Thee in everlasting life. Comfort especially the hearts of those who are bowed down and sorely afflicted by this death, the husband and children of our beloved sister, with the consolations of Thy grace, which alone can afford them help. Let there be light in the midst of this dark night of their grief, and finally bring them, together with the mother for whom they mourn, before Thy presence with exceeding joy. Teach us all to apply our hearts unto wisdom; and when our last hour shall come, be with us in our final distress, that we may look with steadfast faith to Christ, the only Savior of our souls, and, being cleansed by His blood, may lay hold on eternal life. Amen.

9

(At the Death of an Aged Person)

O LORD, almighty God and Father, who of old didst declare: Even to your old age I am He; and even to hoar hairs will I carry you; I have made, and I will bear; even I will carry and will deliver you, we thank Thee that, according to Thy promise, Thou hast for so many years shown our deceased *brother* innumerable proofs of Thy faithfulness and mercy. We thank Thee that Thou hast granted *him* ample time for reflection upon Thy merciful kindness to the fallen children of men and hast given *him* to drink of that well of water which springeth up into everlasting life. And we thank Thee that now Thou hast of Thy mercy delivered *him* from all the labor and sorrow of this present life and received *him* into the rest and peace of Thy heavenly kingdom. Grant unto us all, we beseech Thee, that we may make ready for the unknown hour and for a blessed departure from this world. Enable us to employ well our allotted time and to work while it is day, ere the night cometh when no man can work. And at the last do Thou in love deliver our souls from despair, and let us fall asleep in peace and obtain the crown of everlasting glory; through Jesus Christ, Thy Son, our Lord. Amen.

10

(At the Sudden Death of a Christian)

O ETERNAL GOD, the Lord of life and death, who by a sudden death hast summoned out of time into eternity our Christian *brother,* whom we are about to commit (have committed) to the grave, and by *his* unexpected departure hast grievously afflicted those to whom *he* was near and dear, we beseech Thee, comfort with Thine abundant consolations the hearts of those that mourn, and take them into Thy fatherly care. Enable them to bear this sore dispensation with meek submission to Thy holy will, knowing that all things work together for good to them that love Thee. Grant us grace also that we may be ready either to continue in life or to depart hence, even as Thou hast appointed for us, and cheerfully to bear whatsoever burden Thou mayest be pleased to put upon us. Verily, every man at his best state is altogether vanity. Surely, every man walketh in a vain show. Teach us to watch and pray, and keep us by Thy Spirit, so that we may not be ensnared by the vanities of this time, but finish well our course and pass from death to life everlasting; through Jesus Christ, Thy Son, our Lord. Amen.

❡ Then all shall say

THE LORD'S PRAYER

Our Father who art in heaven.   Hallowed be Thy name.   Thy kingdom come.   Thy will be done on earth as it is in heaven.   Give us this day our daily bread.   And forgive us our trespasses, as we forgive those who trespass against us.   And lead us not into temptation.   But deliver us from evil.   For Thine is the kingdom and the power and the glory forever and ever.   Amen.

❡ Then shall the Minister say or chant

THE BENEDICTION

THE GRACE of our Lord Jesus Christ ✠ and the love of God and the communion of the Holy Ghost be with you all.

❡ Then shall the Congregation say or chant:
Amen.

SILENT PRAYER

AT THE GRAVE

⁋ The Minister, walking before those that bear the body, and approaching the grave, may say:

WE BROUGHT NOTHING into this world, and it is certain we can carry nothing out.

The Lord gave, and the Lord hath taken away; blessed be the name of the Lord.

I would not have you to be ignorant, brethren, concerning them which are asleep, that ye sorrow not, even as others which have no hope. For if we believe that Jesus died and rose again, even so them also which sleep in Jesus will God bring with Him.

They that sow in tears shall reap in joy.

⁋ When the casket is lowered into the grave, a Hymn may be sung.

⁋ Then the Minister shall say:

MAN THAT IS BORN of a woman is of few days and full of trouble. He cometh forth like a flower, and is cut down; he fleeth also as a shadow, and continueth not.

In the midst of life we are in death. Of whom may we seek comfort but of Thee, O Lord, who for our sins art justly displeased?

Yet, O Lord God most holy, O Lord most mighty, O holy and most merciful Savior, deliver us not into the bitter pains of eternal death.

Thou knowest, Lord, the secrets of our hearts; shut not Thy merciful ears to our prayers; but spare us, Lord most holy; O God most mighty, O holy and most merciful Savior, Thou most worthy Judge eternal, suffer us not, at our last hour, for any pains of death to fall from Thee.

So also is the resurrection of the dead. It is sown in corruption; it is raised in incorruption. It is sown in dishonor; it is raised in glory. It is sown in weakness; it is raised in power. It is sown a natural body; it is raised a spiritual body. There is a natural body, and there is a spiritual body. For this corruptible must put on incorruption, and this mortal must put on immortality. So when this corruptible shall have put on incorruption, and this mortal shall have put on immortality, then shall be brought to pass the saying that is written, Death is swallowed up in victory. O Death, where is thy sting? O Grave, where is thy victory? The sting of death is sin; and the strength of sin is the Law. But thanks be to God, which giveth us the victory through our Lord Jesus Christ.

¶ Then, while earth may be cast upon the casket, the Minister shall say:

FORASMUCH as it hath pleased Almighty God, in His wise providence, to take out of this world the soul of our departed *brother*, we therefore commit his body to the ground (to God's acre); earth to earth, ashes to ashes, dust to dust: in the hope of the resurrection to eternal life, through our Lord Jesus Christ, who shall change our vile body that it may be fashioned like unto His glorious body, according to the working whereby He is able even to subdue all things unto Himself.

May God the Father, who has created this body;

May God the Son, who by His blood has redeemed this body together with the soul;

May God the Holy Ghost, who by Baptism has sanctified this body to be His temple, — keep these remains unto the day of the resurrection of all flesh. Amen.

I heard a voice from heaven saying unto me: Write, Blessed

are the dead which die in the Lord from henceforth; yea, saith the Spirit, that they may rest from their labors; and their works do follow them.

I know that my Redeemer liveth and that He shall stand at the Latter Day upon the earth. And though after my skin worms destroy this body, yet in my flesh shall I see God; whom I shall see for myself, and mine eyes shall behold, and not another.

¶ Then may the Minister say one of the following Prayers:

Lᴇᴛ us pray.

1

O Eᴠᴇʀʟᴀsᴛɪɴɢ Gᴏᴅ ᴀɴᴅ Fᴀᴛʜᴇʀ, who art not a God of the dead, but of the living, and unto whom live all that dwell in dust and rest in the chamber of death, we entreat Thee of Thy fatherly goodness, let not the thoughts and the sting of death make us afraid, neither let us be troubled, but graciously keep us in Thy Son in true faith and good conscience, to the end that we may lead a Christian life, prepare for a blessed departure, and finally fall asleep and rest in peace and joy, until Thou wilt open our graves and, by the sound of the trumpet, call us forth again to life; through Jesus Christ, our Lord. Amen.

2

Aʟᴍɪɢʜᴛʏ Gᴏᴅ, who by the death of Thy Son hast overcome sin and death and by His resurrection hast restored innocence and everlasting life, to the end that we should be delivered from the dominion of the devil and that by the power of the same resurrection our mortal bodies should be raised up from the dead unto eternal life in Thy kingdom, grant that with our whole heart we may confidently believe this, and finally, with all Thy saints, be partakers of the joyful resurrection of the just; through the same Jesus Christ, Thy Son, our Lord. Amen.

3

ALMIGHTY AND EVERLASTING GOD, who by Thy Son hast promised us forgiveness of sin and deliverance from everlasting death, strengthen us, we beseech Thee, by Thy Holy Spirit, that our trust in Thy grace in Christ Jesus may daily increase and that with sure confidence we may hold fast the blessed hope that we shall not die, but only sleep, and at the Last Day be raised up unto everlasting life; through the same Jesus Christ, Thy Son, our Lord. Amen.

4

O LORD JESUS CHRIST, who wilt come again in majesty to judge the quick and the dead and call forth all who sleep in the graves, either to the resurrection of life or to the resurrection of condemnation, we beseech Thee to be gracious unto us and to raise us from the death of sin unto the life of righteousness, that, when we shall depart this life, we may rest in Thee and, having been found acceptable in Thy sight, may on the Last Day be raised up to life everlasting and inherit the Kingdom prepared for us from the foundation of the world. To Thee be glory and praise, world without end. Amen.

5

ALMIGHTY GOD, our heavenly Father, who in Thy perfect wisdom and mercy hast ended for Thy departed servant the voyage of this troublous life, grant, we beseech Thee, that we, who are still to continue our course amidst earthly dangers, temptations, and troubles, may evermore be protected by Thy mercy and finally come to the haven of eternal salvation, through Jesus Christ, our Lord. Amen.

7

6

ALMIGHTY GOD, who by the death of Thy Son Jesus Christ hast destroyed death, by His rest in the tomb hast sanctified the graves of Thy saints, and by His glorious resurrection hast brought life and immortality to light through the Gospel, so that all who die in Him abide in joy as to their souls and in hope as to their bodies, receive, we beseech Thee, our unfeigned thanks for that victory over death and the grave which He hath obtained for us and for all who sleep in Him; and keep us, who are still in the body, in everlasting fellowship with all that wait for Thee on earth and with all that are around Thee in heaven, in union with Him who is the Resurrection and the Life, who liveth and reigneth, with Thee and the Holy Ghost, ever one God, world without end. Amen.

℩ Then shall follow the Lord's Prayer.

OUR FATHER who art in heaven. Hallowed be Thy name. Thy kingdom come. Thy will be done on earth as it is in heaven. Give us this day our daily bread. And forgive us our trespasses, as we forgive those who trespass against us. And lead us not into temptation. But deliver us from evil. For Thine is the kingdom and the power and the glory forever and ever. Amen.

℩ Then may a Hymn be sung.

℩ Then shall the Minister say

THE BENEDICTION

THE GRACE of our Lord Jesus Christ ✠ and the love of God and the communion of the Holy Ghost be with you all. Amen.

A READING SERVICE FOR

THE BURIAL
OF THE STILLBORN

(Also for the burial of an unbaptized child)

---✠---

AT THE HOUSE

BELOVED IN THE LORD: Our Savior says in the third chapter of John: Except a man be born of water and of the Spirit, he cannot enter into the Kingdom of God. From this truth it is evident that the Lord has bound His Church to the administration of Holy Baptism. But since the Lord has in no wise bound Himself by this ordinance, this word must be understood of such as have had the opportunity to receive this blessed Sacrament and despised it, but not of such as could not receive Holy Baptism. We may well commend such as could not be baptized to the infinite mercy of God. We may confidently hope that God in His grace has received this child unto Himself for the sake of His Son Jesus Christ.

This comfort is also yours for another reason. This child has been presented to God in the common prayer of the Church, and from His own kind and comforting assurances we know that such prayer in the name of Jesus Christ is heard by Him.

Let this, then, comfort you in your sorrow, and may you humbly and willingly submit to the will of God. The Lord grant that you and all of us may continue steadfast in the faith until in His good season we also attain to eternal blessedness; for the sake of His dear Son Jesus Christ.

Let us pray: O almighty, eternal God and Father, Thou hast given, and Thou hast taken away; as the heavens are higher than the earth, so are Thy thoughts higher than our thoughts; teach us all to trust in Thee, and strengthen the faith of these sorrowing parents (mother), upon whom Thou hast laid this heavy burden.

Help them (her) to receive this affliction from Thy hand as a chastisement unto peace, so that they (she) may confidently believe that Thy ways are goodness and truth. Teach them (her) to depend entirely upon Thy boundless mercy and to maintain this trust that their (her) child, which even before its birth (so soon after its birth) Thou didst call to Thee and which they (she) have (has) for months entrusted to Thy fatherly kindness, was received into Thy heavenly joy even without Baptism, so that it will be returned to them (her) in the resurrection of the righteous. In particular let this affliction serve to keep them (her) in daily repentance, so that they (she) may, in fervent love and true faith, strive for Thy heavenly kingdom, where Thou hast prepared a place also for them (her). Teach us all to number our days, that we may apply our hearts unto wisdom and here in time make diligent use of the means of grace. Grant that we all may be united in Thy heavenly kingdom, through Jesus Christ, Thy Son, our Lord. Amen.

❡ Then shall the Minister say

THE BENEDICTION

THE GRACE of our Lord Jesus Christ ✠ and the love of God and the communion of the Holy Ghost be with you all. Amen.

AT THE GRAVE

❡ When the casket is lowered into the grave, the Minister may say:

THE LORD gave, and the Lord hath taken away; blessed be the name of the Lord.

So also is the resurrection of the dead. It is sown in corruption; it is raised in incorruption. It is sown in weakness; it is raised in power. It is sown a natural body; it is raised a spiritual body. There is a natural body, and there is a spiritual body. For this corruptible must put on incorruption, and this mortal must put on immortality. So when this corruptible shall have put on incorruption, and this mortal shall have put on immortality, then shall be brought to pass the saying that is written, Death is swallowed up in victory. O Death, where is thy sting? O Grave, where is thy victory? The sting of death is sin; and the strength of sin is the Law. But thanks be to God, which giveth us the victory through our Lord Jesus Christ.

❡ The Minister shall then continue:

FORASMUCH as it hath pleased Almighty God, in His wise providence, to take out of this world the soul of this child, we therefore commit its body to the ground; earth to earth, ashes to ashes, dust to dust, in the hope of the resurrection to eternal life, through our Lord Jesus Christ, who shall change our vile body that it may be fashioned like unto His glorious body, according to the working whereby He is able even to subdue all things unto Himself.

Let us pray: Almighty God, who by the death of Thy dear Son hast overcome sin and death and hast redeemed and saved little children no less than others, and hast by His resurrection restored innocence and everlasting life, to the end that we should be delivered from the dominion of the devil, and that by the power of the same resurrection our mortal bodies should be raised up from the dead unto eternal life in Thy kingdom, grant that with our whole heart we may confidently believe this and finally, with all Thy saints, be partakers of the joyful resurrection of the just; through the same Jesus Christ, Thy Son, our Lord. Amen.

℃ Then may follow the Lord's Prayer and the Benediction:

OUR FATHER who art in heaven. Hallowed be Thy name. Thy kingdom come. Thy will be done on earth as it is in heaven. Give us this day our daily bread. And forgive us our trespasses, as we forgive those who trespass against us. And lead us not into temptation. But deliver us from evil. For Thine is the kingdom and the power and the glory forever and ever. Amen.

The grace of our Lord Jesus Christ ✠ and the love of God and the communion of the Holy Ghost be with you all. Amen.

PRAYER AT THE

BURIAL OF A SUICIDE

*When the circumstances are such as to make it possible
for a Christian minister to officiate*

---✠---

MERCIFUL GOD AND FATHER, how unsearchable are Thy judgments, and Thy ways past finding out. We are troubled, yet not distressed; we are perplexed, but not in despair; cast down, but not destroyed. Thou, O Lord, knowest our frame; Thou rememberest that we are but dust. The foolish things of this world and the weak and the base things which are despised hast Thou chosen; that no flesh may glory in Thy sight. Thy strength is made perfect in weakness, and Thy grace in Christ Jesus is sufficient unto us. We pray Thee, grant us grace to make diligent use of Thy Word and Sacrament that we may have the needful strength to resist the wiles of the evil Foe, who seeks to destroy our souls and minds and bodies. Let us never boast of our strength, but ever be mindful of Thy Word. Let him that thinketh he standeth take heed lest he fall. With deep humility we bow before Thee in this hour in which our hearts are burdened with sorrow and grief. We yield ourselves to Thy fatherly guidance with childlike confidence. Thou wilt lead us with Thy right hand and finally receive us unto glory for the sake of Jesus Christ, our only Mediator and Redeemer. Amen.

THE ORDER FOR

THE DEDICATION
OF A DWELLING

✠

⁌ The following Introit may be sung or said:

Our Help is in the name of the Lord, who made heaven and earth.

O Lord, open Thou my lips; and my mouth shall show forth Thy praise.

Show Thy work unto Thy servants and Thine honor unto their children.

Glory be to the Father and to the Son and to the Holy Ghost; as it was in the beginning, is now, and ever shall be, world without end. Amen.

⁌ Then shall the Minister say:

As All Things are sanctified by the Word of God and prayer, let us pray:

O Lord, almighty and eternal God, who hast permitted Thy servants to erect this house, we entreat Thee to enter and abide therein, that the salvation of Thy kingdom may come to all that inhabit it, to the end that Thy name may be hallowed and all glory and worship be given unto Thee from this time forth and even forevermore. Amen.

⁌ Then shall the Minister read a Scripture Lesson, e. g., Luke 19:1-10.

⁌ Then may follow a short Address.

❡ Then shall the Minister say:

LET us pray:

O Lord, holy Father, bless this household, bless their going in; bless them as Thou didst bless the house of Thy patriarchs Abraham, Isaac, and Jacob. O Lord Jesus Christ, who didst say to Thy disciples, When ye enter a house, ye shall greet it and say, Peace be with this house, let Thy peace come upon this house, and bless it with the fullness of Thy grace. O Lord God, Holy Ghost, Thou Spirit of wisdom and truth, of counsel and strength, of knowledge and the fear of God, come to this household with Thy manifold gifts, and sanctify it unto Thy temple and dwelling place. Bless, O Lord, this house and what belongs thereto. Bless its inhabitants with true faith and a godly life, with zeal and faithfulness in Thy service. Bless them with health and strength in body and soul. Let Thy holy angels encamp around this house both day and night. Defend it against all danger, against fire and other calamities. Protect it with Thy mighty hand, and let all that dwell therein live in peace and happiness all the days of their lives. Unto Thee, the Father, the Son, and the Holy Ghost, be praise and glory forevermore. Amen.

❡ Then may the Service close with the Lord's Prayer and the Benediction.

THE FORM FOR

THE OPENING
OF A CONGREGATIONAL
MEETING

───────────── ✠ ─────────────

❡ After the singing of a Hymn the Minister may say:

OUR HELP is in the name of the Lord, who made heaven and earth.

❡ The Assembly shall answer:
Amen.

❡ Then may the Minister say:

THE LORD be with you.

❡ The Assembly shall answer:
And with thy spirit.

❡ Then shall the Minister say:

LET us pray:

1

ALMIGHTY GOD AND LORD, our Father in Christ Jesus, who hast called us to labor in Thy vineyard and without whom we can do nothing, we heartily beseech Thee, vouchsafe unto us Thy gracious presence at this meeting. Enlighten and guide us by Thy Word, that, in all the matters upon which we deliberate, we may know what will promote the best interests of Thy Church and redound to Thy praise. And do Thou bestow Thy blessing upon the measures that we resolve upon in Thy fear. Let Thy Holy Spirit govern and direct our hearts, and let the peace of Thy dear Son dwell in us, that as brethren we may consult peaceably together and as members of the One Head be kindly affectioned one to another with brotherly love, in honor preferring one another, to the end that all we say or do may please Thee; through Jesus Christ, Thy dear Son, our Lord. Amen.

2

O LORD JESUS CHRIST, we are gathered together in Thy name to consult together in peace and amity on important matters relating to the promotion of Thy kingdom. We beseech Thee, therefore, be in the midst of us, according to Thy promise, and grant that we may earnestly desire, wisely search out, truly perceive, and perfectly fulfill those things which are well pleasing in Thy sight, to the praise and glory of Thy name. Amen.

3

DIRECT US, O Lord, in all our doings with Thy most gracious favor, and further us with Thy continual help, that, in all our works begun, continued, and ended in Thee, we may glorify Thy holy name and finally by Thy mercy obtain everlasting life; through Jesus Christ, our Lord. Amen.

4

GOD OF ALL TRUTH AND GRACE, who hast caused the Sun of Righteousness to rise upon a dark and benighted world, be pleased graciously so to illumine the souls of Thy people with the beams of heavenly wisdom that they may continually walk in Thy light and know both to avoid evil and follow after that which is good; through Jesus Christ, our Lord. Amen.

5

ALMIGHTY GOD, direct and govern us by Thy Holy Spirit, guiding us both to devise and to do those things which shall be for the glory of Thy name and the welfare of Thy Church; through Jesus Christ, our Lord. Amen.

6

O LORD, who hast graciously given us Thy Word as a light unto our path, keep us from relying in things spiritual on the judgment of our sin-blinded reason or on the opinions of worldly-minded men; and let us be guided solely by Thine infallible Word, that, turning aside neither to the right hand nor to the left, we may escape the byways of error that imperil the soul, and ever do that which pleaseth Thee and maketh for our salvation, until, having finished our earthly course, we shall enter into everlasting communion with Thee; through Jesus Christ, Thy Son, our Lord. Amen.

❡ Then may one of the Lessons here given be read: Ps. 89:1-18; Psalm 93; Ps. 119:12-24.

❡ The meeting may be closed by the singing of a Hymn, followed by the Lord's Prayer and the Benediction.

LESSONS AND PRAYERS
FOR THE SICK AND THE DYING

✠

AFFLICTIONS AND THEIR USES

LESSONS

Psalm 30   Matt. 8:1-13   John 5:1-14   Heb. 12:1-11
James 1:2-12   1 Pet. 1:3-25

SENTENCES

BEHOLD, happy is the man whom God correcteth; therefore despise not thou the chastening of the Almighty. Job 5:17.

FOR whom the Lord loveth He correcteth, even as a father the son in whom he delighteth. Prov. 3:12.

BEHOLD, I have refined thee; I have chosen thee in the furnace of affliction. Is. 48:10.

MY THOUGHTS are not your thoughts, neither are your ways My ways, saith the Lord. For as the heavens are higher than the earth, so are My ways higher than your ways, and My thoughts than your thoughts. Is. 55:8-9.

I HAVE LOVED thee with an everlasting love; therefore with loving-kindness have I drawn thee. Jer. 31:3.

FOR our light affliction, which is but for a moment, worketh for us a far more exceeding and eternal weight of glory; while we look not at the things which are seen, but at the things which are not seen. 2 Cor. 4:17-18.

BEHOLD, I stand at the door and knock. If any man hear My voice and open the door, I will come in to him, and will sup with him, and he with Me. Rev. 3:20.

HUMBLE YOURSELVES, therefore, under the mighty hand of God, that He may exalt you in due time; casting all your care upon Him; for He careth for you. 1 Pet. 5:6-7.

AS MANY as I love I rebuke and chasten; be zealous therefore and repent. Rev. 3:19.

PRAYERS

LORD GOD, heavenly Father, it hath pleased Thee to visit me with bodily infirmities. I know that Thy love and grace will not permit anything to come upon me unless it is for my good and blessing. Oh, grant that I may rightly receive Thy visitation and that my sickness may be to Thine honor and glory, through Jesus Christ, my Lord and Savior. Amen.

ALMIGHTY AND EVERLASTING GOD, the Consolation of the sorrowful, and the Strength of the weak: let my prayer in tribulation and my cry in distress graciously come before Thee, so that I may see and receive Thy promised help and comfort and deliverance, through Jesus Christ, who is my Savior and my Lord. Amen.

O LORD JESUS, who hast made it my lot to bear the cross give me also an obedient and submissive heart, that I may joy fully take Thy yoke upon me, and willingly follow Thee i every affliction. Amen.

HYMN STANZAS

Beloved, "It is well!"
God's ways are always right;
And perfect love is o'er them all,
Though far above our sight.

Beloved, "It is well!"
Though deep and sore the smart,
The hand that wounds knows how to bind
And heal the broken heart.

Beloved, "It is well!"
Though sorrow clouds our way,
'Twill only make the joy more dear
That ushers in the day.

Beloved, "It is well!"
The path that Jesus trod,
Though rough and strait and dark it be,
Leads home to heaven and God.

Judge not the Lord by feeble sense,
But trust Him for His grace;
Behind a frowning Providence
He hides a smiling face.

His purposes will ripen fast,
Unfolding every hour;
The bud may have a bitter taste,
But sweet will be the flower.

Blind unbelief is sure to err
And scan His work in vain;
God is His own interpreter,
And He will make it plain.

WHAT GOD ordains is always good.
His loving thought attends me;
No poison can be in the cup
That my Physician sends me.
My God is true; Each morn anew
I'll trust His grace unending,
My life to Him commending.

What God ordains is always good.
He is my Friend and Father;
He suffers naught to do me harm,
Though many storms may gather.
Now I may know Both joy and woe,
Some day I shall see clearly
That He hath loved me dearly.

REPENTANCE AND ASSURANCE OF FORGIVENESS

LESSONS

Psalms 32, 51, 130, 25, 77   Matt. 9:1-8
Luke 7:36-50; 15:1-10, 11-32

SENTENCES

SEEK ye the Lord while He may be found; call ye upon Him while He is near. Let the wicked forsake his way, and the unrighteous man his thoughts; and let him return unto the Lord, and He will have mercy upon him, and to our God, for He will abundantly pardon. Is. 55:6-7.

KNOW, therefore, and see that it is an evil thing and bitter, that thou hast forsaken the Lord, thy God, and that My fear is not in thee, saith the Lord God of Hosts. Jer. 2:19.

Remember, O Lord, Thy tender mercies and Thy loving-kindness; for they have been ever of old. Remember not the sins of my youth, nor my transgressions; according to Thy mercy remember Thou me for Thy goodness' sake, O Lord. Ps. 25:6-7.

For the Mountains shall depart, and the hills be removed, but My kindness shall not depart from thee, neither shall the covenant of My peace be removed, saith the Lord, that hath mercy on thee. Is. 54:10.

Surely, He hath borne our griefs and carried our sorrows. He was wounded for our transgressions, He was bruised for our iniquities: the chastisement of our peace was upon Him; and with His stripes we are healed. Is. 53:4-5.

Come unto Me, all ye that labor and are heavy laden, and I will give you rest. Take My yoke upon you, and learn of Me, for I am meek and lowly in heart; and ye shall find rest unto your souls. For My yoke is easy, and My burden is light. Matt. 11:28-30.

Behold the Lamb of God, which taketh away the sin of the world. John 1:29.

God so loved the world that He gave His only-begotten Son, that whosoever believeth in Him should not perish, but have everlasting life. John 3:16.

Neither is there salvation in any other; for there is none other name under heaven given among men whereby we must be saved. Acts 4:12.

God commendeth His love toward us, in that, while we were yet sinners, Christ died for us. Where sin abounded, grace did much more abound. Rom. 5:8, 20.

THIS is a faithful saying and worthy of all acceptation, that Christ Jesus came into the world to save sinners. 1 Tim. 1:15.

THE BLOOD of Jesus Christ cleanseth us from all sin. 1 John 1:7.

PRAYERS

O ALMIGHTY GOD, merciful Father, I, a poor, miserable sinner, confess unto Thee all my sins and iniquities, with which I have ever offended Thee and justly deserved Thy temporal and eternal punishment. But I am heartily sorry for them and sincerely repent of them, and I pray Thee of Thy boundless mercy and for the sake of the holy, innocent, bitter sufferings and death of Thy beloved Son, Jesus Christ, to be gracious and merciful to me, a poor, sinful being. Amen.

O LORD GOD, most merciful Father, through Christ, Thy Son, Thou hast bestowed on me Thy grace, and in Thy Word and through Thy Sacraments Thou hast assured me that, though the mountains should depart and the hills be removed, Thy kindness shall not depart from me, and the covenant of Thy peace shall not be removed. O most faithful Father, I did often forget Thee and neglect Thy covenant; yet Thou didst never forget me, but graciously didst receive me anew. I pray Thee, have mercy on me now. Comfort my heart with the assurance that in sickness and distress I am still Thy dear child. Grant me Christian steadfastness, that I may bear my burden and await Thy help. Thou art my God. Let this be my comfort in life and death. Amen.

LORD JESUS, my dear Savior, how graciously dost Thou call those that labor and are heavy laden unto Thee to give them rest! Behold, I am one that labors and is heavy laden with sickness and misery, sin and iniquity; so, O Lord, fulfill Thy promise and give me rest. Take away my pain and restlessness, and help me. Above all, refresh my poor soul with the forgiveness of sins. Take away from me the burden of my sins, and strengthen in me the faith that Thou hast redeemed me and hast reconciled me to Holy God, so that I may partake of the everlasting rest before Thy throne. Amen.

DEAR GOD AND FATHER, my days are in Thy hand. Do with me as it pleaseth Thee. Only be gracious unto me for Christ's sake. Thou knowest all my sins, which increase the anguish of my heart, but Thou also knowest my Savior, who has atoned for my sins with His blood. Graciously accept this ransom for my sins, and give me the divine assurance through faith that Thou art gracious unto me and that at the end I will most certainly be saved through Jesus Christ, my Savior. Amen.

HYMN STANZAS

I LAY my sins on Jesus,
The spotless Lamb of God;
He bears them all and frees us
From the accursed load.

I lay my griefs on Jesus,
My burdens and my cares;
He from them all releases,
He all my sorrows shares.

I, A SINNER, come to Thee
With a penitent confession;
Savior, mercy show to me,
Grant for all my sins remission.
Let these words my soul relieve:
Jesus sinners doth receive.

Now my conscience is at peace,
From the Law I stand acquitted;
Christ hath purchased my release
And my every sin remitted.
Naught remains my soul to grieve —
Jesus sinners doth receive.

NOT the labors of my hands
Can fulfill Thy Law's demands.
Could my zeal no respite know,
Could my tears forever flow,
All for sin could not atone:
Thou must save, and Thou alone!

PATIENCE UNDER SUFFERING AND TRUST IN GOD'S HELP

LESSONS

Psalms 27, 42, 62, 91, 121   Matt. 7:7-11   Acts 3:1-10
Rom. 8:18-39   2 Cor. 1:3-7; 4:7-18

SENTENCES

COMMIT thy way unto the Lord; trust also in Him; and He shall bring it to pass. Ps. 37:5.

CALL upon Me in the day of trouble; I will deliver thee, and thou shalt glorify Me. Ps. 50:15.

WHY art thou cast down, O my soul? and why art thou disquieted within me? Hope thou in God; for I shall yet praise Him, who is the Health of my countenance and my God. Ps. 42:11.

Whom have I in heaven but Thee? And there is none upon
earth that I desire beside Thee. My flesh and my heart faileth;
but God is the Strength of my heart and my Portion forever.
Ps. 73:25-26.

They that wait upon the Lord shall renew their strength;
they shall mount up with wings as eagles; they shall run and
not be weary, and they shall walk and not faint. Is. 40:31.

Fear thou not, for I am with thee; be not dismayed, for
I am thy God; I will strengthen thee, yea, I will help thee; yea,
I will uphold thee with the right hand of My righteousness.
Is. 41:10.

He that shall endure unto the end, the same shall be saved
(Matt. 24:13); rejoicing in hope, patient in tribulation, continuing instant in prayer (Rom. 12:12).

He hath said, I will never leave thee nor forsake thee, so
that we may boldly say, The Lord is my Helper, and I will not
fear. Heb. 13:5-6.

PRAYERS

O Lord, my God, Thou knowest all my troubles, nor is it
hidden from Thee how restless and cast down my soul frequently is.
Help me, I pray Thee, that I may also, as the psalmist, call on
Thee and from the depth of my heart hope and trust in Thee.
Thou, O God, art my God, my Help and my Hope from my
youth. With Thee nothing is impossible. Thou art able according to Thy mercy to turn my sickness. If it is good for me,
do so. I wholly trust in Thee and wait for Thee. And I shall
yet praise Thee, who art the Health of my countenance and my
God. Amen.

O Most Faithful God, I flee again unto Thee. I have none besides Thee to whom I might turn in my distress. Thou knowest my tribulations, and Thy fatherly heart has pity on me. It might perhaps appear as though now Thou hadst hidden Thy face from me, and Thy mercy might seem to have an end. And I confess that I fully deserve Thy chastisement and am not worthy of Thy help. Yet I am Thy child, saved by the blood of Jesus Christ. Oh, therefore, for Christ's sake, I pray Thee, have mercy on me and help me. Strengthen me through Thy Spirit, that patiently I may await the hour when it shall please Thee to deliver me from my distress either for the present life or for the life to come, according to Thy will. Hear me for Jesus' sake. Amen.

Lord Jesus Christ, give me at all times a patient spirit, willing and ready to wait and pray, that I may not be weary of Thy chastening, but cast my care upon Thee with all cheerfulness and confidence, and ever hope for the best from Thee, who livest and reignest with the Father and the Holy Ghost forever and ever. Amen.

O Lord, heavenly Father, Thou art a faithful God, and sufferest not anyone to be tempted above that he is able to bear: I beseech Thee in my sickness and in my affliction and pain that Thou wouldst not suffer the cross to be too heavy upon me. Strengthen me that I may bear it with patience and nevermore despair of Thy mercy in Jesus Christ, my Lord and Savior. Amen.

HYMN STANZAS

If Thou but suffer God to guide thee
And hope in Him through all thy ways,
He'll give thee strength, whate'er betide thee,
And bear thee through the evil days;
Who trusts in God's unchanging love
Builds on the Rock that naught can move.

Be patient and await His leisure
In cheerful hope, with heart content
To take whate'er thy Father's pleasure
And His discerning love hath sent,
Nor doubt our inmost wants are known
To Him who chose us for His own.

WHAT a Friend we have in Jesus,
All our sins and griefs to bear!
What a privilege, to carry
Everything to God in prayer!
Oh, what peace we often forfeit,
Oh, what needless pain we bear,
All because we do not carry
Everything to God in prayer.

I LEAVE all things to God's direction,
He loveth me in weal and woe;
His will is good, true His affection,
With tender love His heart doth glow.
My Fortress and my Rock is He:
What pleaseth God, that pleaseth me.

OH! for a faith that will not shrink,
Though pressed by many a foe;
That will not tremble on the brink
Of poverty or woe;

That will not murmur nor complain
Beneath the chastening rod,
But in the hour of grief or pain
Can lean upon its God.

PREPARATION FOR DEATH, AND WHEN THE END IS AT HAND

LESSONS

Psalm 90   Job 14:1-5   2 Cor. 5:1-10   Phil. 1:21-30

SENTENCES

THERE remaineth a rest for the people of God. Let us labor, therefore, to enter into that rest. Heb. 4:9, 11.

VERILY, verily, I say unto you: He that heareth My Word and believeth on Him that sent Me, hath everlasting life and shall not come into condemnation, but is passed from death unto life. John 5:24.

I AM now ready to be offered, and the time of my departure is at hand. I have fought a good fight, I have finished my course, I have kept the faith. Henceforth there is laid up for me a crown of righteousness, which the Lord, the righteous Judge, shall give me at that day. 2 Tim. 4:6-8.

THOUGH I walk through the valley of the shadow of death, I will fear no evil, for Thou art with me; Thy rod and Thy staff, they comfort me. Ps. 23:4.

LORD, now lettest Thou Thy servant depart in peace, according to Thy Word; for mine eyes have seen Thy salvation. Luke 2:29-30.

VERILY, I say unto thee, Today shalt thou be with Me in Paradise. Luke 23:43.

LORD JESUS, receive my spirit. Acts 7:59.

PRAYERS

O THOU TRUE SAVIOR, Jesus Christ! Thou art the Lamb of God that takest away the sins of the world, and hast washed and cleansed me in Thy blood. I beseech Thee by Thy bitter Passion, and especially by what Thou didst suffer when Thy soul passed out of the body, have mercy upon my soul in the hour of its departure, and bring me to life everlasting, where Thou livest and reignest forever and ever. Amen.

ALMIGHTY AND ETERNAL GOD, dear, faithful heavenly Father, comfort me, strengthen me, spare me through Thy great mercy. Help me out of all agony and distress. Release me in Thy grace. Take me to Thee, into Thy kingdom. Into Thy hands I commit my soul. Thou hast redeemed me, O Thou faithful God, through the blood of Jesus Christ, my only Lord and Savior. Amen.

LORD, have mercy upon us. Christ, have mercy upon us. Lord, have mercy upon us. Amen.

HYMN STANZAS

JERUSALEM, thou city fair and high,
Would God I were in thee!
My longing heart fain, fain, to thee would fly,
It will not stay with me.
Far over vale and mountain,
Far over field and plain,
It hastes to seek its Fountain
And leave this world of pain.

JESUS, Lover of my soul,
Let me to Thy bosom fly,
While the nearer waters roll,
While the tempest still is high.
Hide me, O my Savior, hide,
Till the storm of life is past;
Safe into the haven guide;
Oh, receive my soul at last!

Other refuge have I none;
Hangs my helpless soul on Thee;
Leave, ah! leave me not alone,
Still support and comfort me.
All my trust on Thee is stayed,
All my help from Thee I bring;
Cover my defenseless head
With the shadow of Thy wing.

ABIDE with me! Fast falls the eventide;
The darkness deepens; Lord, with me abide!
When other helpers fail and comforts flee,
Help of the helpless, oh, abide with me!

MY SAVIOR, be Thou near me
When death is at my door;
Then let Thy presence cheer me,
Forsake me nevermore!
When soul and body languish,
Oh, leave me not alone,
But take away mine anguish
By virtue of Thine own!

Be Thou my Consolation,
My Shield, when I must die;
Remind me of Thy Passion
When my last hour draws nigh.
Mine eyes shall then behold Thee,
Upon Thy cross shall dwell,
My heart by faith enfold Thee.
Who dieth thus dies well!

WHEN the soul is about to depart, the minister may lay his hand on the head of the dying believer and say:

Depart in peace, thou ransomed soul, in the name of God the Father Almighty, who created thee; in the name of Jesus Christ, the Son of the living God, who redeemed thee; in the name of the Holy Ghost, who sanctified thee. Amen.

GRATITUDE FOR RECOVERY

LESSONS

Ps. 103:1-14   Is. 38:9-20   John 5:1-14   Acts 3:1-9

SENTENCES

OFFER unto God thanksgiving, and pay thy vows unto the Most High. Ps. 50:14.

THE LORD is nigh unto all them that call upon Him, to all that call upon Him in truth. He will fulfill the desire of them that fear Him; He also will hear their cry and will save them. Ps. 145:18-19.

THE LORD is good, a Stronghold in the day of trouble; and He knoweth them that trust in Him. Nah. 1:7.

HE giveth power to the faint, and to them that have no might He increaseth strength. They that wait upon the Lord shall renew their strength. Is. 40:29, 31.

PRAYERS

GREAT AND MIGHTY GOD, who bringest down to the grave and bringest up again, we bless Thy wonderful goodness for having turned our heaviness into joy and our mourning into gladness, by restoring this our *brother* to some degree of *his* former health. Blessed be Thy name that Thou didst not forsake *him* in *his* sickness, but didst visit *him* with comforts from above; didst support *him* in patience and submission to Thy will; and at last didst send *him* seasonable relief. Perfect, we beseech Thee, this Thy mercy toward *him*, and prosper the means which shall be made use of for *his* cure, that, being restored to health of body, vigor of mind, and cheerfulness of spirit, *he* may be able to go to Thine house to offer Thee an oblation with great gladness, and to bless Thy holy name for all Thy goodness towards *him*; through Jesus Christ, our Savior, to whom, with Thee and the Holy Spirit, be all honor and glory, world without end. Amen.

I THANK THEE, Lord, Almighty God, that Thou hast visited me as a father and chastened me. Yea, Lord, I am glad that Thou hast humbled me, that I might learn Thy ways. Help now, O Lord, my God, that with renewed health I may also begin a new life. Grant that I may always glorify Thy name, and that Thy praise may be continually found in my mouth. Amen.

HYMN STANZAS

OH, bless the Lord, my soul,
Nor let His mercies lie
Forgotten in unthankfulness
And without praises die!

'Tis He forgives thy sins;
'Tis He relieves thy pain;
'Tis He that heals thy sicknesses
And makes thee young again.

THE LORD hath helped me hitherto
By His surpassing favor;
His mercies every morn were new,
His kindness did not waver.
God hitherto hath been my Guide,
Hath pleasures hitherto supplied,
And hitherto hath helped me.

Help me henceforth, O God of grace,
Help me on each occasion,
Help me in each and every place,
Help me through Jesus' Passion;
Help me in life and death, O God,
Help me through Jesus' dying blood;
Help me as Thou hast helped me!

AT THE SICKBED OF CHILDREN

LESSONS

Psalm 23; 25:1-7; 121   Matt. 9:18, 23-26
Mark 10, 13-15   Titus 3:4-7   Rev. 3:11-12
Explanation of Second Article. (Catechism)

SENTENCES

REMEMBER now thy Creator in the days of thy youth, while the evil days come not, nor the years draw nigh when thou shalt say, I have no pleasure in them. Eccl. 12:1.

FEAR NOT; for I have redeemed thee, I have called thee by thy name; thou art Mine. Is. 43:1.

IN HEAVEN their angels do always behold the face of My Father which is in heaven. Matt. 18:10.

LIKE as a father pitieth his children, so the Lord pitieth them that fear Him. Ps. 103:13.

YE KNOW that ye were not redeemed with corruptible things, as silver and gold, but with the precious blood of Christ, as of a Lamb without blemish and without spot. 1 Pet. 1:18-19.

HE that believeth and is baptized shall be saved. Mark 16:16.

FOR NONE of us liveth to himself, and no man dieth to himself. For whether we live, we live unto the Lord; and whether we die, we die unto the Lord: whether we live, therefore, or die, we are the Lord's. Rom. 14:7-8.

PRAYERS

TENDER JESUS, meek and mild,
Look on me, Thy loving child;
Help me, if it is Thy will,
To recover from all ill. Amen.

ALMIGHTY AND GRACIOUS GOD, whose mercies are over all Thy creatures, look in tender compassion, we beseech Thee, upon Thy servant N., who is sick. Sustain *him* in the trial through which *he* is now passing, and sanctify it to *his* good. Deliver *him* from suffering, and, if in accordance with Thy holy will restore *him* to health and strength, that *he* may joyfully serve Thee in Thy Church, to the honor of Thy name; through Jesus Christ, Thy Son, our Lord. Amen.

O LORD JESUS CHRIST, who camest into this world as a little Child, in want and suffering, look mercifully, we beseech Thee, upon the sick child for whom our prayers are desired; in Thy great love grant *him* relief from all *his* suffering, or else take *him* unto Thyself, where pain shall be no more. Hear us for Thy mercy's sake. Amen.

FOR A CHILD'S RECOVERY FROM SICKNESS

ALMIGHTY GOD AND HEAVENLY FATHER, we give Thee humble thanks because Thou hast been graciously pleased to deliver from *his* bodily sickness the *child* in whose behalf we bless and praise Thy name. Grant, we beseech thee, O gracious Father, that *he*, through Thy help, may both faithfully live in this world according to Thy will, and also may be partaker of everlasting glory in the life to come, through Jesus Christ, our Lord. Amen.

HYMN STANZAS

JESUS, Thy blood and righteousness
My beauty are, my glorious dress;
Midst flaming worlds, in these arrayed,
With joy shall I lift up my head.

JESUS, from Thy throne on high,
Far above the bright blue sky,
Look on us with loving eye;
Hear us, holy Jesus!

Make us brave, without a fear,
Make us happy, full of cheer,
Sure that Thou art always near;
Hear us, holy Jesus!

WHO so happy as I am,
Even now the Shepherd's lamb?
And when my short life is ended,
By His angel host attended,
He shall fold me to His breast,
There within His arms to rest.

THE BLESSING OF THE DYING

LORD JESUS CHRIST, Thou alone art the Door to eternal life;
and if any man enter in by Thee, he shall be saved. We pray
Thee that Thou wouldest open this door of Thy grace to this
our dying *brother* and speedily deliver *him* from the temptation
of sin and the craft and power of the devil. O Lord, do Thou
keep *him* from being lost in the dark valley of the shadow of
death. O Thou Good Shepherd, do not let *him* perish, but receive
the lost sheep as Thy servant. Let Thy Word illumine *his* heart,
help *him* in *his* distress, and show *him* Thy salvation; from the
true faith's comfort do not let *him* fall away; take *his* soul into
Thy hand, and support *him* by Thy grace; let no evil befall *him*,
and thus give *him* eternal life. Amen.

(Here the minister shall lay his hand on the dying person)

FAREWELL then, precious soul, in the name of God the Father,
who so gloriously created thee in His own image; farewell in the
name of God the Son, who so dearly purchased thee and redeemed
thee with His bitter suffering and death; farewell in the name of
God the Holy Ghost, who prepared and sanctified thee as His
temple.

The good and merciful God, who caused poor Lazarus to be
borne into Abraham's bosom and the penitent thief into Paradise,
preserve thee from the devil by the bitter suffering of Jesus Christ,

His dear Son, our Lord and Savior, and guide thee by His dear
angels into the heavenly home, that thou mayest live there with
all the elect in eternal joy and bliss, whither He may help us all
to go when our time here on earth is ended. Amen.

Or:

DEAR SOUL, may God the Father, who so gloriously made
thee in His own image, bless thee! May God the Son, who so
dearly purchased thee by His blood and death, bless thee! May
God the Holy Ghost, who prepared and sanctified thee as His
temple, bless thee!

May the gracious and merciful God by the power of the bitter
suffering and death of Jesus Christ and by the ministry of the
holy angels guide thee into Abraham's bosom, into the eternal
home, that thou mayest live there with all the elect in unspeakable
joy and bliss. May our Lord Jesus Christ be *with* thee to protect
thee, *in* thee to refresh thee, *before* thee to lead thee into heaven,
over thee to bless thee, here in time and hereafter in eternity —
who with the Father and the Holy Ghost liveth and reigneth world
without end. Amen.

BIBLE LESSONS

✠

JOB 14:1-5

MAN that is born of a woman is of few days and full of trouble. He cometh forth like a flower and is cut down; he fleeth also as a shadow and continueth not. And dost Thou open Thine eyes upon such an one and bringest me into judgment with Thee? Who can bring a clean thing out of an unclean? Not one. Seeing his days are determined, the number of his months are with Thee; Thou hast appointed his bounds that he cannot pass.

PSALM 6

O LORD, rebuke me not in Thine anger, neither chasten me in Thy hot displeasure. Have mercy upon me, O Lord, for I am weak; O Lord, heal me, for my bones are vexed. My soul is also sore vexed; but Thou, O Lord, how long? Return, O Lord, deliver my soul; oh, save me for Thy mercies' sake! For in death there is no remembrance of Thee; in the grave who shall give Thee thanks? I am weary with my groaning; all the night make I my bed to swim; I water my couch with my tears. Mine eye is consumed because of grief; it waxeth old because of all mine enemies. Depart from me, all ye workers of iniquity; for the Lord hath heard the voice of my weeping. The Lord hath heard my supplication; the Lord will receive my prayer. Let all mine enemies be ashamed and sore vexed; let them return and be ashamed suddenly.

PSALM 23

THE LORD is my Shepherd; I shall not want. He maketh me to lie down in green pastures; He leadeth me beside the still waters. He restoreth my soul; He leadeth me in the paths of righteousness for His name's sake. Yea, though I walk through the valley of the shadow of death, I will fear no evil, for Thou art with me; Thy rod and Thy staff, they comfort me. Thou preparest a table before me in the presence of mine enemies; Thou anointest my head with oil; my cup runneth over. Surely goodness and mercy shall follow me all the days of my life; and I will dwell in the house of the Lord forever.

PSALM 25

UNTO THEE, O Lord, do I lift up my soul. O my God, I trust in Thee; let me not be ashamed, let not mine enemies triumph over me. Yea, let none that wait on Thee be ashamed; let them be ashamed which transgress without cause. Show me Thy ways, O Lord; teach me Thy paths. Lead me in Thy truth and teach me; for Thou art the God of my salvation; on Thee do I wait all the day. Remember, O Lord, Thy tender mercies and Thy loving-kindnesses; for they have been ever of old. Remember not the sins of my youth nor my transgressions; according to Thy mercy remember Thou me for Thy goodness' sake, O Lord. Good and upright is the Lord; therefore will He teach sinners in the way. The meek will He guide in judgment, and the meek will He teach His way. All the paths of the Lord are mercy and truth unto such as keep His covenant and His testimonies. For Thy name's sake, O Lord, pardon mine iniquity; for it is great. What man is he that feareth the Lord? Him shall He teach in the way that he shall choose. His soul shall dwell at ease, and his seed shall inherit the earth. The secret of the Lord is with them that fear Him, and He will show them His covenant. Mine eyes are ever toward the Lord; for He shall pluck my feet out of the net. Turn Thee unto me and have mercy upon me; for I am desolate and afflicted. The troubles of my heart are enlarged; oh, bring Thou me out of my distresses. Look upon mine affliction and my pain, and forgive all my sins. Consider mine enemies, for they are many; and they hate me with cruel hatred. Oh, keep my soul and deliver me, let me not be ashamed; for I put my trust in Thee. Let integrity and uprightness preserve me; for I wait on Thee. Redeem Israel, O God, out of all his troubles.

PSALM 27

THE LORD is my Light and my Salvation; whom shall I fear? The Lord is the Strength of my life; of whom shall I be afraid? When the wicked, even mine enemies and my foes, came upon me to eat my flesh, they stumbled and fell. Though a host should encamp against me, my heart shall not fear; though war should rise against me, in this will I be confident. One thing have I desired of the Lord, that will I seek after: that I may dwell in the house of the Lord all the days of my life to behold the beauty of the Lord and to inquire in His Temple. For in the time of trouble He shall hide me in His pavilion; in the secret of His tabernacle shall He hide me; He shall set me up upon a rock. And now shall mine head be lifted up above mine enemies round about me. Therefore will I offer in His tabernacle sacrifices of joy; I will sing, yea, I will sing praises unto the Lord. Hear, O Lord, when I cry with my voice: have mercy also upon me and answer me. When Thou saidst, Seek ye My face, my heart said unto Thee, Thy face, Lord, will I seek. Hide not Thy face far from me; put not Thy servant away in anger. Thou hast been my Help; leave me not, neither forsake me, O God of my salvation. When my father and my mother forsake me, then the Lord will take me up. Teach me Thy way, O Lord; and lead me in a plain path because of mine enemies. Deliver me not over unto the will of mine enemies; for false witnesses are risen up against me, and such as breathe out cruelty. I had fainted unless I had believed to see the goodness of the Lord in the land of the living. Wait on the Lord; be of good courage, and He shall strengthen thine heart. Wait, I say, on the Lord.

PSALM 30

I WILL EXTOL Thee, O Lord; for Thou hast lifted me up and hast not made my foes to rejoice over me. O Lord, my God, I cried unto Thee, and Thou hast healed me. O Lord, Thou hast brought up my soul from the grave; Thou hast kept me alive, that I should not go down to the pit. Sing unto the Lord, O ye saints of His, and give thanks at the remembrance of His holiness. For His anger endureth but a moment; in His favor is life; weeping may endure for a night, but joy cometh in the morning. And in my prosperity I said, I shall never be moved. Lord, by Thy favor Thou hast made my mountain to stand strong; Thou didst hide Thy face, and I was troubled. I cried to Thee, O Lord; and unto the Lord I made supplication. What profit is there in my blood when I go down to the pit? Shall the dust praise Thee? Shall it declare Thy truth? Hear, O Lord, and have mercy upon me; Lord, be Thou my Helper. Thou hast turned for me my mourning into dancing; Thou hast put off my sackcloth and girded me with gladness, to the end that my glory may sing praise to Thee and not be silent. O Lord, my God, I will give thanks unto Thee forever.

PSALM 32

BLESSED is he whose transgression is forgiven, whose sin is covered. Blessed is the man unto whom the Lord imputeth not iniquity, and in whose spirit there is no guile. When I kept silence, my bones waxed old through my roaring all the day long. For day and night Thy hand was heavy upon me; my moisture is turned into the drought of summer. I acknowledged my sin unto Thee, and mine iniquity have I not hid. I said, I will confess my transgressions unto the Lord; and Thou forgavest the iniquity of my sin. For this shall everyone that is godly pray unto Thee in a time when Thou mayest be found; surely in the floods of

great waters they shall not come nigh unto him.   Thou art my
Hiding Place; Thou shalt preserve me from trouble; Thou shalt
compass me about with songs of deliverance.   I will instruct thee
and teach thee in the way which thou shalt go; I will guide thee
with Mine eye.   Be ye not as the horse or as the mule, which have
no understanding; whose mouth must be held in with bit and
bridle, lest they come near unto thee.   Many sorrows shall be to
the wicked; but he that trusteth in the Lord, mercy shall compass
him about.   Be glad in the Lord and rejoice, ye righteous; and
shout for joy, all ye that are upright in heart.

PSALM 51

HAVE MERCY upon me, O God, according to Thy loving-
kindness; according unto the multitude of Thy tender mercies
blot out my transgressions.   Wash me throughly from mine
iniquity, and cleanse me from my sin.   For I acknowledge my
transgressions, and my sin is ever before me.   Against Thee, Thee
only, have I sinned and done this evil in Thy sight, that Thou
mightest be justified when Thou speakest, and be clear when Thou
judgest.   Behold, I was shapen in iniquity, and in sin did my
mother conceive me.   Behold, Thou desirest truth in the inward
parts; and in the hidden part Thou shalt make me to know
wisdom.   Purge me with hyssop, and I shall be clean; wash me,
and I shall be whiter than snow.   Make me to hear joy and gladness, that the bones which Thou hast broken may rejoice.   Hide
Thy face from my sins, and blot out all mine iniquities.   Create
in me a clean heart, O God; and renew a right spirit within me.
Cast me not away from Thy presence, and take not Thy Holy
Spirit from me.   Restore unto me the joy of Thy salvation, and
uphold me with Thy free Spirit.   Then will I teach transgressors
Thy ways; and sinners shall be converted unto Thee.   Deliver
me from bloodguiltiness, O God, Thou God of my salvation;

and my tongue shall sing aloud of Thy righteousness. O Lord, open Thou my lips; and my mouth shall show forth Thy praise. For Thou desirest not sacrifice; else would I give it; Thou delightest not in burnt offering. The sacrifices of God are a broken spirit; a broken and a contrite heart, O God, Thou wilt not despise. Do good in Thy good pleasure unto Zion; build Thou the walls of Jerusalem. Then shalt Thou be pleased with the sacrifices of righteousness, with burnt offering and whole burnt offering; then shall they offer bullocks upon Thine altar.

PSALM 90:1-12, 13-17

Lord, Thou hast been our Dwelling Place in all generations. Before the mountains were brought forth or ever Thou hadst formed the earth and the world, even from everlasting to everlasting, Thou art God. Thou turnest man to destruction and sayest, Return, ye children of men. For a thousand years in Thy sight are but as yesterday when it is past, and as a watch in the night. Thou carriest them away as with a flood; they are as a sleep; in the morning they are like grass which groweth up. In the morning it flourisheth and groweth up; in the evening it is cut down and withereth. For we are consumed by Thine anger, and by Thy wrath are we troubled. Thou hast set our iniquities before Thee, our secret sins in the light of Thy countenance. For all our days are passed away in Thy wrath; we spend our years as a tale that is told. The days of our years are threescore years and ten; and if by reason of strength they be fourscore years, yet is their strength labor and sorrow; for it is soon cut off, and we fly away. Who knoweth the power of Thine anger? Even according to Thy fear, so is Thy wrath. So teach us to number our days, that we may apply our hearts unto wisdom.

Return, O Lord, how long? And let it repent Thee concerning Thy servants. Oh, satisfy us early with Thy mercy, that we may rejoice and be glad all our days. Make us glad according to the days wherein Thou hast afflicted us, and the years wherein we have seen evil. Let Thy work appear unto Thy servants and Thy glory unto their children. And let the beauty of the Lord, our God, be upon us; and establish Thou the work of our hands upon us; yea, the work of our hands, establish Thou it.

PSALM 91

He that dwelleth in the secret place of the Most High shall abide under the shadow of the Almighty. I will say of the Lord, He is my Refuge and my Fortress: my God, in Him will I trust. Surely He shall deliver thee from the snare of the fowler and from the noisome pestilence. He shall cover thee with His feathers, and under His wings shalt thou trust; His truth shall be thy shield and buckler. Thou shalt not be afraid for the terror by night; nor for the arrow that flieth by day; nor for the pestilence that walketh in darkness; nor for the destruction that wasteth at noonday. A thousand shall fall at thy side, and ten thousand at thy right hand; but it shall not come nigh thee. Only with thine eyes shalt thou behold and see the reward of the wicked. Because thou hast made the Lord, which is my Refuge, even the Most High, thy habitation, there shall no evil befall thee, neither shall any plague come nigh thy dwelling. For He shall give His angels charge over thee to keep thee in all thy ways. They shall bear thee up in their hands, lest thou dash thy foot against a stone. Thou shalt tread upon the lion and adder; the young lion and the dragon shalt thou trample under feet. Because he hath set his love upon Me, therefore will I deliver him; I will set him on high, because he hath known My name. He shall call upon Me, and I will answer him; I will be with him in trouble; I will deliver him and honor him. With long life will I satisfy him and show him My salvation.

PSALM 103:1-14, 15-22

BLESS THE LORD, O my soul; and all that is within me, bless His holy name. Bless the Lord, O my soul, and forget not all His benefits; who forgiveth all thine iniquities; who healeth all thy diseases; who redeemeth thy life from destruction; who crowneth thee with loving-kindness and tender mercies; who satisfieth thy mouth with good things, so that thy youth is renewed like the eagle's. The Lord executeth righteousness and judgment for all that are oppressed. He made known His ways unto Moses, His acts unto the Children of Israel. The Lord is merciful and gracious, slow to anger, and plenteous in mercy. He will not always chide, neither will He keep His anger forever. He hath not dealt with us after our sins, nor rewarded us according to our iniquities. For as the heaven is high above the earth, so great is His mercy toward them that fear Him. As far as the east is from the west, so far hath He removed our transgressions from us. Like as a father pitieth his children, so the Lord pitieth them that fear Him. For He knoweth our frame; He remembereth that we are dust.

As for man, his days are as grass; as a flower of the field, so he flourisheth. For the wind passeth over it, and it is gone, and the place thereof shall know it no more. But the mercy of the Lord is from everlasting to everlasting upon them that fear Him, and His righteousness unto children's children to such as keep His covenant, and to those that remember His commandments to do them. The Lord hath prepared His throne in the heavens, and His kingdom ruleth over all. Bless the Lord, ye His angels, that excel in strength, that do His commandments, hearkening unto the voice of His word. Bless ye the Lord, all ye His hosts, ye ministers of His that do His pleasure. Bless the Lord, all His works, in all places of His dominion: bless the Lord, O my soul.

PSALM 121

I WILL LIFT UP mine eyes unto the hills from whence cometh my help.   My help cometh from the Lord, which made heaven and earth.   He will not suffer thy foot to be moved; He that keepeth thee will not slumber.   Behold, He that keepeth Israel shall neither slumber nor sleep.   The Lord is thy Keeper; the Lord is thy shade upon thy right hand.   The sun shall not smite thee by day nor the moon by night.   The Lord shall pre- serve thee from all evil; He shall preserve thy soul.   The Lord shall preserve thy going out and thy coming in from this time forth and even forevermore.

PSALM 130

OUT OF THE DEPTHS have I cried unto thee, O Lord.   Lord, hear my voice; let Thine ears be attentive to the voice of my supplications. If Thou, Lord, shouldest mark iniquities, O Lord, who shall stand?   But there is forgiveness with Thee, that Thou mayest be feared.   I wait for the Lord, my soul doth wait, and in His Word do I hope.   My soul waiteth for the Lord more than they that watch for the morning; I say, more than they that watch for the morning.   Let Israel hope in the Lord; for with the Lord there is mercy, and with Him is plenteous redemption. And He shall redeem Israel from all his iniquities.

MATT. 9:18-19, 23-26

WHILE HE SPAKE these things unto them, behold, there came a certain ruler and worshiped Him, saying, My daughter is even now dead; but come and lay Thy hand upon her, and she shall live.   And Jesus arose and followed him, and so did His disciples. . . .   And when Jesus came into the ruler's house and saw the minstrels and the people making a noise, He said unto them, Give place: for the maid is not dead, but sleepeth.   And they laughed Him to scorn. But when the people were put forth, He went in and took her by the hand, and the maid arose. And the fame hereof went abroad into all that land.

MATT. 25:1-13

THEN shall the kingdom of heaven be likened unto ten virgins which took their lamps and went forth to meet the bridegroom. And five of them were wise, and five were foolish. They that were foolish took their lamps and took no oil with them; but the wise took oil in their vessels with their lamps. While the bridegroom tarried, they all slumbered and slept. And at midnight there was a cry made, Behold, the bridegroom cometh; go ye out to meet him! Then all those virgins arose and trimmed their lamps. And the foolish said unto the wise, Give us of your oil; for our lamps are gone out. But the wise answered, saying, Not so, lest there be not enough for us and you; but go ye rather to them that sell, and buy for yourselves. And while they went to buy, the bridegroom came; and they that were ready went in with him to the marriage. And the door was shut. Afterward came also the other virgins, saying, Lord, Lord, open to us! But he answered and said, Verily I say unto you, I know you not. Watch therefore; for ye know neither the day nor the hour wherein the Son of Man cometh.

MARK 10:13-16

AND they brought young children to Him that He should touch them; and His disciples rebuked those that brought them. But when Jesus saw it, He was much displeased and said unto them, Suffer the little children to come unto Me, and forbid them not; for of such is the Kingdom of God. Verily I say unto you, Whosoever shall not receive the kingdom of God as a little child, he shall not enter therein. And He took them up in His arms, put His hands upon them, and blessed them.

LUKE 7:11-17

AND it came to pass that He went into a city called Nain; and many of His disciples went with Him and much people. Now, when He came nigh to the gate of the city, behold, there was a dead man carried out, the only son of his mother, and she was a widow; and much people of the city was with her. And when the Lord saw her, He had compassion on her and said unto her, Weep not. And He came and touched the bier; and they that bare him stool still. And He said, Young man, I say unto thee, Arise. And he that was dead sat up and began to speak. And He delivered him to his mother. And there came a fear on all, and they glorified God, saying, That a great prophet is risen up among us; and, That God hath visited His people. And this rumor of Him went forth throughout all Judea and throughout all the region round about.

JOHN 11:20-27

THEN Martha, as soon as she heard that Jesus was coming, went and met Him; but Mary sat still in the house. Then said Martha unto Jesus, Lord, if Thou hadst been here, my brother had not died. But I know that even now, whatsoever Thou wilt ask of God, God will give it Thee. Jesus saith unto her, Thy brother shall rise again. Martha saith unto Him, I know that he shall rise again in the resurrection at the last day. Jesus said unto her, I am the Resurrection and the Life; he that believeth in Me, though he were dead, yet shall he live; and whosoever liveth and believeth in Me shall never die. Believest thou this? She saith unto Him, Yea, Lord, I believe that Thou art the Christ, the Son of God, which should come into the world.

JOHN 14:1-6

LET not your heart be troubled. Ye believe in God, believe also in Me. In My Father's house are many mansions; if it were

l you. I go to prepare a place for you.
a place for you, I will come again and
that, where I am, there ye may be also.
w, and the way ye know. Thomas saith
ow not whither Thou goest; and how
Jesus saith unto him, I am the Way, the
o man cometh unto the Father but by Me.

JOHN 16:16-23

, and ye shall not see Me; and again a little
Me, because I go to the Father. Then said
nong themselves, What is this that He saith
, and ye shall not see Me; and again a little
Me; and, Because I go to the Father? They
is this that He saith, A little while? We
saith. Now, Jesus knew that they were
and said unto them, Do ye inquire among
aid, A little while, and ye shall not see Me;
le, and ye shall see Me? Verily, verily, I say
shall weep and lament, but the world shall
be sorrowful, but your sorrow shall be turned
A woman, when she is in travail, hath sorrow, because
come; but as soon as she is delivered of the child, she
no more the anguish, for joy that a man is born into
And ye now therefore have sorrow; but I will see
d your heart shall rejoice, and your joy no man taketh
from you. And in that day ye shall ask Me nothing.

ACTS 9:36-42

Now there was at Joppa a certain disciple named Tabitha,
which by interpretation is called Dorcas; this woman was full
of good works and almsdeeds which she did. And it came to

pass in those days that she was sick and died; whom when they had washed, they laid her in an upper chamber. And forasmuch as Lydda was nigh to Joppa, and the disciples had heard that Peter was there, they sent unto him two men, desiring him that he would not delay to come to them. Then Peter arose and went with them. When he was come, they brought him into the upper chamber; and all the widows stood by him weeping, and showing the coats and garments which Dorcas made while she was with them. But Peter put them all forth and kneeled down and prayed; and turning him to the body, said, Tabitha, arise. And she opened her eyes; and when she saw Peter, she sat up. And he gave her his hand and lifted her up and, when he had called the saints and widows, presented her alive. And it was known throughout all Joppa; and many believed in the Lord.

1 COR. 15:20-28, 35-49, 50-58

BUT now is Christ risen from the dead and become the First Fruits of them that slept. For since by man came death, by Man came also the resurrection of the dead. For as in Adam all die, even so in Christ shall all be made alive. But every man in his own order: Christ the First Fruits; afterward they that are Christ's, at His coming. Then cometh the end, when He shall have delivered up the Kingdom to God, even the Father; when He shall have put down all rule and all authority and power. For He must reign till He hath put all enemies under His feet. The last enemy that shall be destroyed is death; for He hath put all things under His feet. But when He said, All things are put under Him, it is manifest that He is excepted which did put all things under Him. And when all things shall be subdued unto Him, then shall the Son also Himself be subject unto Him that put all things under Him, that God may be all in all.

But some man will say, How are the dead raised up, and

with what body do they come?   Thou fool, that which thou sowest is not quickened, except it die; and that which thou sowest, thou sowest not that body that shall be, but bare grain, it may chance of wheat or of some other grain; but God giveth it a body as it hath pleased Him, and to every seed his own body.   All flesh is not the same flesh; but there is one kind of flesh of men, another flesh of beasts, another of fishes, and another of birds.   There are also celestial bodies and bodies terrestrial; but the glory of the celestial is one, and the glory of the terrestrial is another.   There is one glory of the sun, and another glory of the moon, and another glory of the stars; for one star differeth from another star in glory. So also is the resurrection of the dead.   It is sown in corruption, it is raised in incorruption; it is sown in dishonor, it is raised in glory; it is sown in weakness, it is raised in power; it is sown a natural body, it is raised a spiritual body.   There is a natural body, and there is a spiritual body.   And so it is written, The first man, Adam, was made a living soul; the last Adam was made a quickening spirit.   Howbeit, that was not first which is spiritual, but that which is natural, and afterward that which is spiritual.   The first man is of the earth, earthy; the second Man is the Lord from heaven.   As is the earthy, such are they also that are earthy; and as is the heavenly, such are they also that are heavenly.   And as we have borne the image of the earthy, we shall also bear the image of the heavenly.

Now, this I say, brethren, that flesh and blood cannot inherit the Kingdom of God; neither doth corruption inherit incorruption. Behold, I show you a mystery: We shall not all sleep, but we shall all be changed, in a moment, in the twinkling of an eye, at the last trump; for the trumpet shall sound, and the dead shall be raised incorruptible, and we shall be changed.   For this corruptible must put on incorruption, and this mortal must put on immortality. So when this corruptible shall have put on incorruption, and this mortal shall have put on immortality, then shall be brought to pass the saying that is written, Death is swallowed up in victory. O Death, where is thy sting? O Grave, where is thy victory? The sting of death is sin, and the strength of sin is the Law. But thanks be to God, which giveth us the victory through our Lord Jesus Christ. Therefore, my beloved brethren, be ye steadfast, unmovable, always abounding in the work of the Lord, forasmuch as ye know that your labor is not in vain in the Lord.

2 COR. 5:1-10

We know that if our earthly house of this tabernacle were dissolved, we have a building of God, an house not made with hands, eternal, in the heavens. For in this we groan, earnestly desiring to be clothed upon with our house which is from heaven; if so be that, being clothed, we shall not be found naked. For we that are in this tabernacle do groan, being burdened; not for that we would be unclothed, but clothed upon, that mortality might be swallowed up of life. Now He that hath wrought us for the selfsame thing is God, who also hath given unto us the earnest of the Spirit. Therefore we are always confident, knowing that, whilst we are at home in the body, we are absent from the Lord (for we walk by faith, not by sight); we are confident, I say, and willing rather to be absent from the body and to be present with the Lord. Wherefore we labor, that, whether present or absent, we may be accepted of Him. For we must all appear before the judgment seat of Christ, that everyone may receive the things done in his body, according to that he hath done, whether it be good or bad.

1 THESS. 4:13-18 .

But I would not have you to be ignorant, brethren, concerning them which are asleep, that ye sorrow not, even as others which have no hope. For if we believe that Jesus died and rose

again, even so them also which sleep in Jesus will God bring with
Him. For this we say unto you by the word of the Lord, that
ये which are alive ▮nd remain unto the coming of the Lord shall
not prevent them ▮hich are asleep. For the Lord Himself shall
descend from heaven ▮ with a shout, with the voice of the archangel,
and with the trump ▮ of God; and the dead in Christ shall rise first.
Then we which are ▮ alive and remain shall be caught up together
with them in the ▮ouds to meet the Lord in the air; and so shall
we ever be with ▮e Lord. Wherefore comfort one another with
these words.

2 TIM. 4:6-8

▮w ready to be offered, and the time of my
▮l. I have fought a good fight, I have finished
▮ kept the faith; henceforth there is laid up for
▮eousness, which the Lord, the righteous Judge,
▮t day; and not to me only, but unto all them
▮ppearing.

1 PET. 1:3-9

▮e God and Father of our Lord Jesus Christ,
▮ His abundant mercy hath begotten us again
▮ by the resurrection of Jesus Christ from the
▮nce incorruptible and undefiled and that fadeth
▮ in heaven for you, who are kept by the power
▮ith unto salvation ready to be revealed in the
▮ ye greatly rejoice, though now for a season,
▮ heaviness through manifold temptations, that
the trial of your faith, being much more precious than of gold that
perisheth, though it be tried with fire, might be found unto praise
and honor and glory at the appearing of Jesus Christ: whom
having not seen, ye love; in whom, though now ye see Him not,
yet believing, ye rejoice with joy unspeakable and full of glory,
receiving the end of your faith, even the salvation of your souls.

REV. 7:9-17

AFTER this I beheld, and, lo, a great multitude, which no man could number, out of all nations and kindreds and people and tongues, stood before the throne and before the Lamb, clothed with white robes, and palms in their hands; and cried with a loud voice, saying, Salvation to our God which sitteth upon the throne, and unto the Lamb. And all the angels stood round about the throne, and about the elders and the four beasts, and fell before the throne on their faces and worshiped God, saying, Amen: Blessing and glory and wisdom and thanksgiving and honor and power and might be unto our God forever and ever. Amen. And one of the elders answered, saying unto me, What are these which are arrayed in white robes, and whence came they? And I said unto him, Sir, thou knowest. And he said to me, These are they which came out of great tribulation, and have washed their robes and made them white in the blood of the Lamb. Therefore are they before the throne of God and serve Him day and night in His temple; and He that sitteth on the throne shall dwell among them. They shall hunger no more, neither thirst any more; neither shall the sun light on them nor any heat. For the Lamb which is in the midst of the throne shall feed them, and shall lead them unto living fountains of waters; and God shall wipe away all tears from their eyes.

A PASTOR'S
DAILY PRAYER

✠

O ALMIGHTY GOD, merciful Father, I, a poor, miserable sinner, confess unto Thee all my sins and iniquities; especially do I acknowledge my indolence in prayer, my neglect of Thy Word, and my seeking after good days and vainglory. But I am heartily sorry for them and sincerely repent of them; and I pray Thee, of Thy boundless mercy and for the sake of the holy, innocent, bitter sufferings and death of Thy beloved Son, forgive me all my sins, and be gracious and merciful to me. Yea, cleanse me through Thy Spirit by the blood of Jesus Christ, and give me more and more power and willingness to strive after holiness, for Thou hast called me that I should be holy and blameless before Thee in love.

I thank Thee also, O faithful God, for my family, my wife and children, and for all my relatives. Thou hast given them to me purely out of fatherly, divine goodness and mercy, without any merit or worthiness in me. Preserve them in good health, and give me their daily bread; but above all keep them in Thy grace and in the true confession of Thy name unto the end.

Thou, O God of all grace and mercy, hast also called me, a poor unworthy sinner, to be a servant of Thy Word and hast placed me into that office which preaches the reconciliation and hast given me this flock to feed. In and by myself I am wholly incompetent to perform the work of this great office; and, therefore, I pray Thee, make me an able minister of Thy Church. Give me Thy Holy Spirit, the Spirit of wisdom and knowledge, of grace and prayer, of power and strength, of courage and joyfulness, of sanctification and the fear of God. Fill me with the right knowledge, and open my lips that my mouth may proclaim the honor of Thy name. Fill my heart with a passion for souls and with skillfulness to give unto each and every sheep or lamb entrusted to my care what is due unto it at the proper time. Give me at all times sound advice and just works; and wherever I overlook something or in the weakness of my flesh speak or act wrongly, do Thou set it aright, and help that no one may through me suffer harm to his soul.

Glory and honor, praise and thanks be unto Thee, God, Father, Son, and Holy Ghost, for all the mercy and faithfulness Thou hast shown to this congregation. Thy Word has not returned unto Thee void, but Thou hast here gathered a people that knows Thee and fears Thy name. Give me Thy Holy Spirit, that I may at all times see the good things in this congregation and praise and thank Thee for them. Bless Thy Word in the future, that it may preserve the believers in Thy grace, convert those that are not yet Thine, and bring back the erring and delinquent. Gather Thy people as a hen gathereth her chickens under her wings, and be Thou a wall of fire round about Thy congregation.

Graciously take into Thy fatherly care the sick and the needy, all widows and orphans, and all who are in any trouble, temptation, anguish of labor, peril of death, or any other adversity. Comfort them, O God, with Thy Holy Spirit, that they may patiently endure their afflictions and acknowledge them as a manifestation of Thy fatherly will. Preserve their soul from faintheartedness and despondency, and help that they may seek Thee, the great Physician of their souls. And if any pass through the valley of the shadow of death, suffer them not, in the last hour, for any pain or fear of death, to fall away from Thee, but let Thine everlasting arms be underneath them, and grant them a peaceful departure and a happy entrance into Thine eternal kingdom.

Furthermore, I pray Thee, Thou wouldst at all times fill the offices of this congregation and its societies with upright, honest, and sincere men and women, who have the welfare of their congregation at heart and are able to help me in my office with their counsel and their deeds. Unite their hearts with me in love for the truth; give them the spirit of prayer for me and for their congregation, so that we may in unity and harmony build Thy kingdom in this place.

And since hypocrites and ungodly people are often found within the visible church organization, I pray Thee, do not permit Satan to disrupt this congregation through such or to hinder the efficiency of my office. If there are such in our midst, let Thy Word be like unto a hammer upon their hearts of stone. Have patience with them; but if they persist in their unbelief, hypocrisy, and wickedness, do Thou reveal them, so that they may be put forth from Thy congregation. Give me a forgiving heart towards all, and help me, especially for their sake, to speak and act cautiously.

Preserve and keep the youth of our Church from falling away and joining the world, and keep them from the many sins of youth. Thou, O Lord, knowest how difficult it is to lead the young on the right paths and to divide the Word of Truth with respect to them; do Thou, therefore, give me particular wisdom and skill to be stern without estranging their hearts, and mild and charitable without strengthening them in frivolity and unruliness.

Mercifully bless the education of the children that they may grow up in Thy fear to the praise of Thy name. I commend unto Thee also the Christian day school. Hinder and frustrate all enemies of this institution. May I ever regard and accept it as a precious gift of God! Grant our congregation able and consecrated teachers. Give them joy in their arduous ministry and true success. Bless also the work of our Sunday school teachers, and help them to lead the little ones into the Savior's loving arms.

To Thy grace and mercy I also commend all my brethren in office. Arrest and suppress all discord and dissension. Give me a brotherly heart towards all and true humility, and help me to bear with patience their casual weakness or deficiencies. Grant that they also may act as true brethren toward me.

Keep and preserve our whole Synod, its teachers and officers, true to Thy Word. Cause the work of our Synod to grow. Guard and protect all members of Synod against sinful ambitions, dissension, and indifference in doctrine and practice. Bless all higher institutions of learning, our colleges, seminaries, and university. Accompany all missionaries on their dangerous ways, and help them to perform their work. Gather the elect from all nations into Thy holy Christian Church, and bring them at last into Thy Church Triumphant in heaven.

Grant also health and prosperity to all that are in authority in our country, especially to * the President and Congress of the United States, the Governor and Legislature of this State, and to all Judges and Magistrates.

* For Use in the British Empire	Her Majesty the Queen of the British Commonwealth of Nations, the Governor-General and the Prime Minister of our Dominion, as well as the Premier of our Province, and all Governments and Parliaments, and all Judges and Magistrates.

Endue them with grace to rule after Thy good pleasure, to the maintenance of righteousness and to the hindrance and punishment of wickedness, that we may lead a quiet and peaceable life in all godliness and honesty.

Hear me, most merciful God, in these my humble requests, which I offer up unto Thee in the name of Jesus Christ, Thy Son, our Lord, to whom, with Thee and the Holy Ghost, be all honor and glory, world without end. Amen.